CAMP FIRE
GIRL

MY STORY OF SURVIVAL AND RECOVERY FROM THE DEADLY 2018 WILDFIRE CALLED THE CAMP FIRE

BY
ERIN ELLIS RHATIGAN RN

ISBN: 979-8-89109-650-9 - paperback

ISBN: 979-8-89109-651-6 - ebook

TABLE OF CONTENTS

RECOVERY

THE END

ACKNOWLEDGMENTS

I want to dedicate this book to my husband, BJ, my mother, Sue, and the rest of my family. Bridget Rood, my brave and strong beyond her wildest imagination stepdaughter; Bill Rood, our loving and fierce son-in-law who broke land speed records to get home to all of us; and our wonderful and smart grandsons, Billy Rood and Mark Rood; we are so proud of you both. Without the love, prayers, and support of my family, I would not be here today. Thank you also to my Aunt Pat and Uncle Raleigh Wills, who supported us when we had nowhere else to go.

The family includes more than just the people you are born into, but also those chosen by us to be as close as family. Therefore, I am also dedicating this book to Sandy Sabagh, my sister from a different mister, and her late significant other, Richard Kent, who was a wonderful friend and adopted brother to my husband and me. Thank you for welcoming us into your home for the much-needed escape from our trauma and stress.

I would also like to acknowledge all the men, women, and children affected by the Camp Fire and all the resolute men and women working at Adventist Health on November 8, 2018. You all know who you are; we will never forget that day for as long as we live. Thank you for all you did for us and each other. You are all heroes to me and the people of Paradise.

I have a special thank you to the first responders for CAL Fire; if it were not for you, I would not be here today. And for everyone who put their lives second over their neighbors—because of all of you, there were no more than 85 fatalities that day. May God bless you and keep you all safe and happy.

INTRODUCTION

Wildfires have the potential to harm property, livelihoods, and human health. 2018, on November 8, the deadliest and most expensive wildfire in California history occurred. It happened in Butte County, California. Eighty-five people died, eighteen thousand structures were destroyed, 153,336 acres were burned, and 52,000 people were displaced in less than twelve hours.[1] I was nearly eighty-six, but thank God, I was one of those survivors instead, and this is my story.

As you read my account of survival, I would like you to try to put yourself in my shoes for a moment and see if you, the reader, can understand what it was like living through such a deadly wildfire. It is one of the most terrifying and life-changing events ever imaginable. In less than twelve hours, 95% of your town is destroyed, your neighbors are gone, and you don't know if they are alive or dead. You have nothing but clothes on your back, and your cell phone, and the smoke is so thick it is as dark as night. Only by trying to imagine yourself living through such a horrific event will you understand how important it is to plan for such a life-altering disaster. No one ever expects to go through such a terrible event, yet over 60,000 communities in the United States are at risk for wildfires due to Wildland Urban Interface (WUI). Wildland urban interface, or WUI, is just what it sounds like. It's where communities of people live in an area that used to be all trees and animals but is now shared with people as well.[2]

The WUI areas continue to grow by approximately 2 million acres per year, with the United States having the most significant number of houses in the WUI listed below in order:

1. California 2. Texas 3. Florida 4. North Carolina 5. Pennsylvania[3]

Fire-related threats are increasing annually. According to the National Oceanic and Atmospheric Administration, between 1980 and 2021, the United States had 20 wildfire events that caused more than $1 billion in damage. Over the past few decades, the United States has routinely spent more than $1 billion annually to fight wildfires, including $2.3 billion in 2020. These efforts have resulted in the deaths of more than 1,000 firefighters since 1910. Even in communities far downwind, wildfire smoke has been directly linked to poor air quality that can lead to significant health effects and costs to society (emergency department visits, hospital admissions, and deaths, often due to respiratory ailments. In fact, at the time of this book's writing, over 450 fires are burning in Canada, and over 250 of them are still out of control and causing the worst air quality on the east coast of America and Europe.[4]

No one person can prevent a wildfire from happening or prevent the readers of this book from having to go through one. Still, by reading this book, I hope that the reader will have a much better understanding of what a wildfire looks like from an eyewitness account, how preparing for a wildfire can be the key to survival, and how preplanning by individuals and communities can prevent or mitigate the damages and losses our community of Paradise is now experiencing.

BEFORE THE FIRE

CHAPTER I

THE TOWN OF PARADISE

My name is Erin Ellis Rhatigan, and I am a sixty-two-year-old registered nurse who currently lives in Keaau, Hawaii, on the Big Island of Hawaii with my family. I have been a registered nurse for the last forty years. Before living in Hawaii, I lived in Auburn, California, with my husband BJ and my mother Sue; before Auburn, we all lived together in a twenty-four hundred square foot home in a small town called Paradise in the Sierra foothills of California, and this is our story of survival and recovery after the Camp Fire that destroyed our town of Paradise, California in 2018.

My husband BJ, short for Bernard Joseph, and I had been married for twenty-one years, and we were living in Benicia, California when we visited his daughter, my stepdaughter, Bridget, her husband Bill, our Grandsons Billy and Mark in Magalia, California, near Paradise in 2017.

Paradise, California, is about twelve miles east of Chico, California. It was the summer hunting grounds of the Maidu Indian tribe, but when the California gold rush happened around 1848, many people flocked to the area to try their hand at prospecting. Families began moving into the area in the 1850s to the sixties, and lumber mills also began around that time. The population grew steadily over the years until, in 1979, the population grew to over 20,000 people. The people of Paradise decided to incorporate in 1979 as the town of Paradise.[5]

Paradise had a community hospital, pharmacy, library, restaurants, and shopping. It was a small community of about twenty-seven thousand people who were knowledgeable about each other's businesses like any other small community.

Paradise had an apple orchard that had been there for generations where you could bring the family to pick apples and have fun getting to know your family and neighbors. It had a family that made candy there for generations and that everyone went to for their Christmas treats. There was a hardware store where you could find anything you needed to build, repair, or fix your house. The hardware store employees were always there to help you with any project you were working on. If you needed help with your projects, they were there to make it easier.

The Paradise post office was so lovely that even if you had to wait in line, you enjoyed talking to your neighbors until it was your turn, and your mail carrier knew your name and waved to you when they drove down the street. The same went for the banks, their employees, the restaurant owners, and their waitstaff. It had three grocery stores, one for every socioeconomic group. It also had a Big K-Mart, a Big 5 Sporting Goods, and several antique stores. There was a Black Bear Diner, a Sushi restaurant, at least three other diners, and a fine-dining establishment with a full bar. There were three motels, the most popular being the Best Western on Clark Road.

Paradise had one community hospital, Feather River Hospital, three skilled nursing facilities, board and care homes, doctor's offices, clinics, and pharmacies for medical care. Many clinics, pharmacies, and other medical facilities were owned and operated by Feather River Hospital, the town's leading source of employment. It even had a senior housing apartment community or two, one of which was located on the hospital property.

Of course, Paradise had its homeless population and, like many communities, had drug problems. Still, the entire community usually knew who needed services and did what they could to help.

Bridget and I are as close as possible; she was one of my bridesmaids at my wedding to her father when she was twelve and I was 30. I've known her since she was seven. I love her like my daughter, and I was at the birth of each of her children. I love them all as if they were my own flesh and blood.

Whenever my husband BJ and I visited our daughter and her family, we always got the question, "So when are you moving here?" We would laugh it off and say as soon as we both retire. We would look at open houses that our daughter wanted us to see when we visited, but we never saw any we felt were the right house for us until one of our visits in March 2017.

My husband and I were visiting our daughter Bridget and her family when Bridget suggested we see some open houses in Magalia and Paradise. So, we decided to see some of the houses available. We went to see a few houses that our daughter Bridget saw in the newspaper were having open houses. We liked the location and

5

price of two houses but were not ready to commit yet. My husband and I went home after that visit, and we couldn't get the houses and the price of the houses out of our heads. I had been thinking about trying to work part-time and gradually ease into retirement, so we considered moving to Magalia or Paradise, California. We would be near our daughter and our Grandchildren, and we would be able to buy a bigger home for the money than we ever could in the East Bay Area where we live in Benicia, California. So, we started going up to Paradise every weekend to look for houses.

CHAPTER 2

LIVING IN PARADISE

In April 2018, we finally found a house we were happy with, and I found a job that allowed me to work three days a week with medical benefits at Feather River Hospital. I would be a case manager or discharge planner for the hospital. While I wouldn't be retired, I was easing into retirement by only working three days a week instead of five.

My husband and I put our house in Benicia, California, on the market and were surprised at how slowly it took to sell. The real estate market was hot, so we figured selling would only take a few weeks. Boy, were we wrong? We put our house on the market in May of 2018, and the house didn't sell until July. My husband and I couldn't understand it. We kept wondering if maybe we were not supposed to sell.

My mom was older and living alone in Walnut Creek, California. BJ and I did not like the idea of her living so far away when we moved to Paradise, California, in case something happened and she needed assistance. Mom didn't drive at that point, so getting to the store or the doctor would be a chore if we were not nearby to help her. So, we asked Mom to move to Paradise and live with us. The house we chose and bought in Paradise had a basement apartment that we selected with the idea that Mom would come live with us but still have her own apartment.

The first night we brought Mom to Paradise to see the house and to choose a temporary room until we could make any changes she wanted to her new apartment, she fell and broke her wrist. This prevented her from being able to go back to her old apartment in Walnut Creek to pack up her belongings. Mom needed help to bathe, dress, and perform all her activities of daily living because the wrist she broke was her right wrist, and she was right-handed.

My husband had to go to her apartment and pack up all her belongings, including six generations of family history-related documents, letters, antiques, and pictures she was carrying for the entire family. Mom had become the family historian, and as such, she had six generations of family memorabilia in her one-bedroom senior apartment. It was quite a feat and one he did not take lightly.

Finally, on July 5, 2018, we were all living under the same roof. I was working at the hospital, and my husband, who was retired, was busy fixing the downstairs apartment for Mom to move into. On the weekends, I was busy unloading boxes and assembling our new house to make it a home. I was looking forward to having our first Thanksgiving in our new home and having Bridget, Bill, Billy, and Mark over for Thanksgiving dinner. I planned on having a huge Thanksgiving dinner with the whole family gathered around one table. I even bought a large new dining room table that would hold all of us around it.

Our house was twenty-four hundred square feet, with most of the living space on the first floor and the apartment downstairs in the basement area. It had a huge balcony looking out over the canyon's view. We had about twenty-five sugar pine trees around the house's front and back yards. My mom said, "I can't believe we live in a beautiful forest. We are so lucky."

The address of our house in Paradise was 7053 Molokai Drive. We joked between Mom, BJ, and me that we lived in Paradise, not in Hawaii, but in California. We enjoyed going over to our daughter's house for dinner on the weekends and having the boys at our house throughout the summer whenever Bridget or Bill was not home because they had to work. Having our grandson trick-or-treat at our house on Halloween was so much fun. It was a grandparent's dream come true.

CHAPTER 3

RURAL VS. URBAN LIVING

L ife in Paradise was vastly different from the urban life we were all used to before coming here. We now live in a rural forest setting, complete with everything that goes along with living in a forest. We had birds, squirrels, frogs, many trees, deer, skunks, raccoons, bears, and the occasional mountain lion. The first morning we were in our new house, my husband BJ was sitting on the front porch drinking his coffee when he spotted a large cat, which he thought was someone's very large pet cat, running through the yard across the street. He said it stopped and cleaned its face as cats do. He was amazed at how big the neighbor cat was and could not wait to tell Mom and me when we woke up later that morning.

My mom was the next one up that morning, and she was sitting on the back deck drinking her coffee, watching the animals and birds, and admiring the new place we now lived in. She had been told about the large house cat that BJ had seen earlier that morning and was on the lookout for it and anything else that she would see. Suddenly, she spotted what she thought was a large dog running across the neighbor's yard next door and then spotted the long tail. She yelled to my husband, "BJ, that wasn't a house cat you saw earlier; it's a mountain lion." My husband ran to see it again and said, "Yes, that's what I saw earlier." Mom told him, "That was no house cat. It was a mountain lion." She later told me this story and that the mountain lion gradually meandered into the canyon behind our house. I was glad to have missed that little welcome to the neighborhood after I got up a bit later. All I could think of was, "We're not in the city anymore, that's for sure." It was good that we had no pets living with us then.

Our days were simple enough but quite different than when they lived in the city. I got up early and watched the news to hear the weather for the day and to see if there were any issues we needed to be aware of "on the ridge." That is what our town of Paradise was now known as to those of us living there. It was life on the ridge. The town of Paradise is a town on the edge of two canyons. It's on the ridge line above the canyons.

The mornings consisted of getting up, eating breakfast, drinking coffee, showering, and dressing for work at the hospital. I would get into my car and open the garage door because we never knew what beastie was outside. It could be our neighbor's dog, a skunk, a raccoon, a bear, or a mountain lion. One never knew. I would drive to work; it took me all five or ten minutes, and I had an electric plug-in hybrid car, so I never got out of electric mode before getting to the hospital parking lot. It was wonderful. My little Chevy Volt was a great car, which sure turned heads up there on the ridge.

I spent my day working hard but loving what I did. I was back to doing patient care, maybe not doing bedside care, but collaborating with patients and families all the same. I was once again living and working in my community. It felt good to be caring for my fellow community members and neighbors. I loved seeing them healthy in the community and knowing I had a hand in making that happen.

On my days off, I would take Mom to her doctor's and occupational therapy appointments to help her rehabilitate from her broken wrist. I also went grocery shopping and unpacked what felt like hundreds of boxes. My husband and I rearranged our furniture and shopped for new appliances or furniture in the many consignment shops to help make our new house a home.

I had the most exciting stories but was careful never to give too much detail. I always cringed when we heard a helicopter overhead, hoping it was not a forest fire somewhere in the area. We knew there was the possibility of a forest fire, but we never really thought it would happen. There had been a couple of scares with the possible evacuation of the hospital in the past, but it was never much of a real threat. We knew it could happen but never thought it really would. We were in a drought in California, and all the plants and trees were dry as a tinder box, but we kept our 100 feet around our house defensible space, so we figured everything would be okay.

As the season changed, I was leaving the hospital when it was dark, so I never knew what awaited me in the parking lot. One time, there was a six-point buck near my car, and we both scared each other. I nodded to him, and he nodded back, and we went our separate ways. It was so strange. I felt like I was becoming one with nature.

We met all the neighbors one day, and they all said that if we needed anything, we just needed to let them know, and they would all help. "We help each other out here on the ridge." We finally felt like we were part of a community. I even volunteered to have our department's Christmas party at our house because it was perfect for entertaining. I was looking forward to life on the ridge.

We unpacked our last box and had our house put together how we wanted it. Mom was moved into her new apartment and was contented living in, as she called it, "our lovely forest house." We had fun watching the birds build nests and watched the squirrels chase each other around the pine trees in our backyard. We even had one squirrel who adopted us as its people and would watch us through the windows while sitting on the fence top. We had heard of deer coming to our backyard to nibble on the blackberry bushes. We even had a family of bears who would do the same thing. We were part of a beautiful new forest community of people and animals.

THE FIRE

CHAPTER 4

THE FIRE STARTS

November 8, 2018, started with me being angry and upset with my husband for something stupid. I had a fever and felt like I had the flu, so I was grumpy and easily annoyed. It was overcast and cool but not cold. As I contemplated not going to work and calling in sick, I realized it was too short of notice for anyone to be called to replace me. It was my last day of work for the week, so I decided to stay away from people as much as possible, wear a mask if I needed to be around anyone, and tough it out and go on to work. I could always go home if I felt worse.

I watched the news while eating a light breakfast of toast, and I got dressed for the day. The news was interesting in that the meteorologist said it would be an extra windy day and that PG&E (Pacific Gas and Electric Company) was sending out notifications about possibly shutting off the power to the area because of the expected high winds. They were worried that the high winds might blow down a live power line and cause a fire. This warning from PG&E had been repeated on the news for two days, but they still had not shut off the power. All I could think of was that it would be my luck for the power to be shut off before I could get a shower and my hair dried. I got ready for work at about eight o'clock instead of my usual eight-thirty and decided to go in a little early.

As I was backing out of my garage, I noticed there seemed to be fog in our area. It seemed a little early in the year for fog, but since we were new to the area, that seemed plausible. I also noticed the smell of wood smoke in the air, and I thought someone must be having a fire in the fireplace. Lucky them. It smelled lovely and seemed like a beautiful fall morning. The traffic was heavy on Skyway, one of the main roads out of the town, but it was because I left earlier than usual, so this may be what the traffic is like at this time of the morning.

As I arrived at the hospital's parking lot, I noticed the fog was getting thicker, and as I got out of my car, I saw white stuff blowing around in the air. I realized the white stuff was ash in the air and immediately realized that ash meant a forest fire somewhere nearby. I jumped back into my car and pulled up the Cal Fire website on my cell phone to see where the fire was and how close it was to us in Paradise. The fire was in a place called Pulga off Camp Creek Road. I had no idea where that was in relation to the hospital or the town of Paradise. I called my husband at home and asked him where Pulga was, and he said, "Oh, that is at least ten miles away from us. We are fine." I was relieved and explained that there was a forest fire there, and I asked him if he would please check on it to ensure it was not getting closer to us and keep me updated. He said he would but that I should not worry and have a nice day. I told him I would and that I would see him tonight.

At this point, explaining how fires in California get their names is important. They are named after the name of the street they start on. In the case of the Camp Fire, it started on Camp Road in Pulga, hence the name of the Camp Fire. The reader needs to understand this because calling this fire the Camp Fire seems silly and insulting unless you understand how California wildfires get their names.

As I walked to the door of the hospital that I usually go into near the physical therapy department, I noticed smoke billowing out in huge plumes behind the hospital. I said aloud when I saw the smoke billowing, "Shit, that can't be good." Then I saw a sign on the door that said, "Keep this door closed to keep out the fire smoke." Another co-worker and I entered the door, closing it behind us immediately. We were greeted by a co-worker who said a forest fire was approaching the hospital, and we may be evacuating it.

I immediately went right to my office to see what was happening. I didn't even waste time clocking in. I remember talking to my director, Teri, and asking her what was happening. She explained that a fire was coming up the canyon, and we were preparing for possible evacuation. She asked me to manage a phone call for her of a patient who had just been discharged from the hospital but was needing antibiotics on his way to evacuate the fire.

I answered the telephone and said, "Hello, how can I help?" The patient's daughter said, "I'm here with my father in Concow, and he needs to pick up his antibiotics on the way out of town. He was just discharged from the hospital. We're evacuating from the fire." I then asked her if she could get to the Skyway Hospital pharmacy on the way out of town, and she said, "Yes, but we need his antibiotics to be there when we get there." I explained to her that they would be there. She said, "We have to go. The fire is here, but we still need the antibiotics." I told her, "Just go. Do not worry about the antibiotics. We will figure out how to get them for you. Just get your father and your family out of there now."

I then hung up the phone, called the pharmacy on Skyway, gave them all the information, and said I would have the hospital doctor fax over a prescription but that the family was on their way and would stop in on their way out of town to evacuate the fire. The pharmacist said it was fine and not to worry. They had the antibiotics and would fill the prescription. I called one of our hospitalist doctors working that day and asked him to send the prescription to the Skyway pharmacy for this patient who had been discharged earlier. The doctor said he was already working on it and would send it as soon as he finished writing it.

CHAPTER 5

EVACUATION

Just as I hung up the telephone from the hospitalist, our office door burst open, and a nurse ran in and asked where the case management director was. She said, "We're evacuating the hospital, and we need the director at the hospital command center right away." Teri followed the nurse to the command center and said, "I'll be back as soon as possible." One of my co-workers and a hospital social worker, Christia, said, "Erin, I'm scared." I said, "I'm scared too, but we'll be all right. We need to take a deep breath, pray, and do what we must to evacuate the patients and ourselves." We hugged each other and said a quick prayer. We had no sooner said "amen" than our boss, Teri, burst through the door to let us know we were evacuating the patients from the hospital. Our job would be to prepare the patient charts to go with them to Oroville Hospital or Enloe in Chico. We should split up, and each take a unit in the hospital and get to work.

I called my husband at home to tell him what was happening, that we were evacuating the hospital, and to let him know where I would be. He said, "I am evacuating your mom and me because the fire is here at our house."

I replied, "Oh my God, okay. Grab the important papers box, your laptop, my laptop, and Mom, and I'll see you and Mom in Chico at Enloe Hospital as soon as I arrive. Be careful. I love you. See you soon."

After hanging up with BJ, I told Christia I could take the surgical floor and the ICU, and she volunteered to take the cardiac and OB units. As we quickly made our way to our respective units, we met up with another two case management staff coming in, Myra and Josh. I relayed the situation and told Myra and Josh where each of us was going. Myra took the medical surgical unit, and Josh went to the ER. Once all the units were covered, Teri left us to return to the command center. I said goodbye to my co-workers, saying, "Good luck and God Bless, and I'll see you over at Enloe in a little while." They said their goodbyes and said see you there too.

Once I arrived at the surgical unit, I asked the unit secretary or unit clerk how I could help her get the charts ready for transport with the patients. She said she was copying the charts and putting them in large envelopes to get them ready to go. I said I would help her by copying them, and she agreed. Just as I started to take some papers out of the first chart, the nursing supervisor, Jeff, came by and said the fire was headed for the hospital, and we had forty-five minutes before it was here. At that point, I said, "No time to copy the charts. We'll take them with us. I told the unit clerk that we could sort out where Oroville and Enloe wanted the charts and in what form once we got everyone where they were supposed to be and safe. We could transport the charts in a car or ambulance. She thought that was a fine idea and agreed to oversee getting the charts down to the emergency department on the gurney.

Once that was settled, I began helping to evacuate patients. I noticed we were going back into rooms that had already been evacuated and asked the nurses on the unit, "Where are your room evacuation signs?" The nurses looked at me questioningly and finally said, "Oh yeah, we're supposed to be putting them on the doors of the patient rooms." I explained to the nurses before me, "The signs go on the closed doors of the patient rooms we have already evacuated so we don't keep going back into them repeatedly."

We helped patients who were ambulatory get into cars. We helped them into either their family and friends' cars or even into one of the hospital staff members' cars to be driven by staff to either Oroville or Enloe Hospital in Chico. If a patient could not get into a car and was bed-bound or gurney-bound, we helped them to the emergency department into a waiting ambulance. The ambulances then took these patients to either Enloe or Oroville Hospital.

After finishing with the surgical unit, I hurried to the ICU down the hall to see if I could help them. When I reached the ICU, the unit clerk told me he did not need any help, and the last patient was being wheeled down the hall to the ER on a gurney.

Once all the patients were either evacuated or awaiting an ambulance, my director told me to go ahead and head to Enloe Hospital in Chico, where we would help settle our patients into the new hospital and help notify the families of the patients where their loved ones were. Terri and I left about the same time, and both of us had to find our cars in the parking lot amongst all the other cars. It may seem like an easy task, but it was not. It was dark as night outside the hospital. Even though it was ten thirty in the morning, it looked like it was ten thirty at night outside because of the smoke. On the way out of the hospital, I thought to grab a flimsy yellow surgical mask, the only mask I could find. I hoped the mask would help with the smoke until I could get into my car.

CHAPTER 6

ARMAGEDDON

The air was so thick with smoke that it was hard to breathe, and if you breathed too deeply, your throat hurt, and your lungs started to burn. I turned around, looking for my car several times because I had left through an unfamiliar door outside of the emergency room, and it was dark as night with the smoke so thick it blotted out the sun. I had also only been working at Feather River for four months on the day of the fire. I still needed to learn my way around the hospital. The emergency room parking lot was a hive of activity with cars going in different directions trying to flee the fire.

I stopped and asked one gentleman in the parking lot if he knew which way to the employee parking lot from where we were, and he said, "I'm sorry, I don't know where it is. I'm just here picking up family." So, I looked around and found what I thought was the path to the employee parking lot, and finally stumbled onto my car. I was very much out of breath when I got into it, and I was hoping not to have an asthma attack before I got out of the parking lot. As soon as I got into my car, I closed all the vents to the outside and turned on the air conditioning. I slowly edged my way out of the employee parking lot.

As I pulled out of the parking lot, there were so many cars trying to do the same thing I was—evacuating the area. It reminded me of the shopping center parking lot on Black Friday. We sat impatiently, waiting our turn to exit, hoping to escape the area as quickly as possible. It was stop-and-go traffic, I crept along at what seemed like one to two miles an hour. I was trying to maintain my calm and not panic. I finally made it to Pentz Road, and I turned right on Pentz like I always did to go down Billy Road to Skyway. I was planning to go down Skyway to Chico.

Suddenly, the cars ahead of me on the opposite side of the road began honking their horns and yelling out their car windows, "There's fire on the road! You can't get through that way! Turn around. Go the other direction." So, as soon as it was safe, I pulled over to the opposite side of the road and made a fast U-turn. As I did my turn, the wind was howling hard, and the trees overhead were wiping around with leaves and debris flying everywhere. It was still dark as night, with the only light visible were the lights from car headlights. Suddenly, without warning, a large, thick branch from an oak tree hit the roof of my car and bounced down the passenger side of my Chevy Volt. It landed down on the ground next to my car with a thud. All I could think of at that point was, "That's going to leave a heck of a scratch or a dent."

I gently pulled out onto Pentz Road. Heading toward Highway 70, I planned on going down Pentz to the highway and then over toward Chico. Instead, I was directed by a police officer to go down Pearson Road. I turned right onto Pearson Road and began a slow ninemile-an-hour creep down that road. The road was so dark that we had to have our lights on to see anything on the road. As I got further down Pearson Rd, it was so dark it seemed like ten thirty at night rather than ten thirty in the morning. I looked around the road and noticed the trees on either side were catching fire. Embers were blowing in the wind and across the road and into the sugar pine trees, catching them on fire one right after the other. I never realized until it happened that a pine tree could explode. I saw a tree on the right side of the road explode into flames like a Roman candle. When it gets hot, the pine pitch explodes from inside the tree trunk to the outside. It sounds like when a burning log in the fireplace pops, but one hundred times louder. Who knew? Not me. I do now, though.

Once the trees started exploding, the propane tanks around the nearby houses all began to explode. It sounded like a war zone, with everything catching fire and exploding around me. That's when I really got scared. I realized this wasn't good and wondered if I would make it out of there alive. Until then, I was scared but still felt I would make it out of there okay.

The next thing that happened was my cell phone rang, and it was my stepdaughter, Bridget. She said, "Erin, it's Bridget. I'm evacuating the skilled nursing facility, and I'm scared. I'm driving down Skyway toward Chico with several other people from the facility in my car." told her, "Bridget, I know you're scared, but you will be all right. Just keep heading down Skyway to Chico; you will be okay. Your dad and my mom are heading to Enloe Hospital and should be there by the time you get to Chico. I have to go now, honey. I'm on Pearson Road about halfway down, and fire is surrounding me.

I have to try to get out of here now. I love you. Please tell everyone I love them." I hung up. It was one of the hardest things I had to do so far that day.

Next, a yellow Volkswagen bug caught fire on the opposite side of the road from me and had its gas tank explode. I watched it catch fire, and as if in slow motion, I watched the gas tank blow out the side of the car. Luckily for me, the car must have been low on gas because it didn't explode far from the car.

After the Volkswagen exploded and after saying goodbye to my stepdaughter and the rest of my family through her, I began praying. My prayers were frantic at that point, and I was screaming them to God all alone in my car. "God, I don't want to die like this. I don't want to die like this. God, I don't want to die!"

Suddenly, I heard a voice that was not my normal inward voice inside my head saying, "Finally. I was waiting to hear you say that. Unlock your car doors." I knew without a doubt that it was the voice of God, and I began to talk to Him. I started crying and laughing simultaneously, saying, "Oh yeah, thank you, God, someone might need to get into my car to escape." So, I unlocked all my doors in case someone needed to get in. I was so glad to realize God was with me and I wasn't alone.

Not even two minutes after I unlocked my doors, my passenger door opened, and a woman I had never met started to jump into my car. She said, "I'm sorry, but my truck behind you caught fire and burned up. I just threw my bottle of water all over me and ran for the nearest car." I told her, "Get in, and let's get the hell out of here," and she did. I asked her if she was okay and if she got burned, and she said she thought the hair on her arms got a little singed, but otherwise, she was fine, scared. It was not until much later in the day that we realized the tops of both of her ears had second-degree burns, and she had no hair left on either of her forearms.

I decided to try to lighten the mood that had gotten very intense, and I said, "My name is Erin Rhatigan. What's your name?" She replied, "Hi Erin, nice to meet you. I'm Karen, Karen Davis." "It is nice to meet you, too." I noticed she was wearing dark blue scrubs, so I asked, "Where in the hospital do you work?"

"I work the night shift on the surgical floor. I'm an RN in the surgical unit. I was getting off work when the fire started. How about you? Where do you work?" I was wearing street clothes and a lab coat over them. I told her, "I'm one of the RN Case Managers at the hospital. I came to work today not knowing anything about the fire until I got here and saw the ash blowing around and smoke billowing out from behind the hospital."

Suddenly, we both realized we had been stopped behind the car in front of us, a Honda Pilot, for a while, and we were not moving. I looked at Karen, and she looked at me and said, "Do you mind if I pray?" I said, "Not at all. I'll pray along with you." We did. Karen had also been on her cell phone with her daughter Wendy, so Karen, her daughter, and I all started praying to God, asking Him to get us out of there. "Dear Heavenly Father, if it is your will, please get us out of here. We know that You can do anything, and we ask that You please get us out of this fire and to safety. In Your son Jesus Christ's name. Amen."

Karen's daughter asked me if there was anyone, she could call for me to let them know where I was. I said, "Yes. Please call my husband BJ Rhatigan and tell him where I am, that I will get there as soon as possible, and that I love him." Then I gave her BJ's phone number, and we hung up so she could call him for me. I could not call BJ because I was working hard to escape the fire area and was concentrating on driving. I was laser-focused on my concentration, focusing all my efforts on trying to escape the inferno.

No sooner had we hung up on Karen's daughter Wendy than we saw bright lights coming up the road on my left out of the dark. It was a bulldozer. A Cal Fire bulldozer. I had no idea what he was doing there, but then, out of the dark from the opposite direction, came a Cal fireman in his firefighting gear with a bullhorn telling all of us to stay in our cars and that we were going to pull off the road a little way ahead on a small pull out. We were all going to turn around and head back to the hospital. He said, "The bulldozer driver is going to push all the burned-out cars off the road so we can get through, and we will caravan back to the hospital to shelter in place. A fire truck is there hosing down the hospital, and the hospital has not burned, so we should be safe until help arrives." Sheltering in place means precisely what it says. It means staying in the safest area that one can find and staying there either until help arrives or until you can leave safely to go to a safer location.

It took a few minutes for all of us to pull off the road onto the pull-out and turn around. There was fire surrounding us on all sides. As I was driving up to the turnaround point, I saw in my mind's eye angels with their wings outstretched over the front of my car, and I heard and saw in my mind's eye angels on the roof of my car and all around the road seemed to be protecting us. I have never had any visions before in my life, but this time, it was as clear as watching a movie on TV. I was in awe at what I was seeing. Then we turned off the road and turned around.

We played bumper cars while turning around because the area we had to turn around was so small, and there was fire burning in the woods surrounding it, but we made it. It was funny, though, because we were all so profoundly sorry when we bumped into one another's cars that we mouthed "I'm sorry" to each other as we bumped into each other. We were as polite as possible while banging the heck out of each other's cars. None of us were going extremely fast, but we were not being incredibly careful either. We were scared and trying to get out of there alive. We waited a few minutes while the bulldozer driver moved all the burned-out cars out of the way, then we did exactly what we were told to do and caravanned back to the hospital with the Cal Fire truck in the lead.

As I drove back up Pearson Road, I had my windshield wipers going and the wiper fluid squirting over my windshield to keep the embers that were flying across my windshield from catching fire and burning my car up with Karen and me inside. It was hot in that car. It felt like an oven and sweat rolled down my back and neck. I also had on a cotton shirt and a pair of polyester business pants with my white lab coat, and Karen had on scrubs; we were sweating like crazy. Neither of us wore a mask the whole time we were in the car. It was just too hot to wear it. As I pulled into the hospital parking lot, water poured out of a break in the water main. I drove through the fountain of water, hoping that if any embers had been burning on my car, the water would put the fire out so I could drive my car again, if necessary, later.

As Karen and I climbed out of my car, I could not believe my little Chevy Volt kept us alive and did not burn up around us. Karen ran to my side of the car and hugged me, saying, "We made it, Erin. We're alive!" And she headed toward the entrance to the hospital. I looked around at where we were and quietly said so she did not hear me, "Yes, but for how long?" I knew the fire was still burning, and we were in the middle of the fire zone.

CHAPTER 7

SHELTER IN PLACE

The fire was still burning around the hospital's perimeter, and firefighters were frantically hosing the hospital buildings and outbuildings to keep the embers blowing all around from catching the hospital on fire. I could hear propane tanks blowing up in the near distance and saw embers flying around with ash. We were safe for now, and I had to go to the bathroom, something fierce. Karen and I and several other hospital employees were entering the hospital. The hospital's interior was dark; it smelled like smoke, and we all had to get our cell phone flashlights lit to see our way through the hospital and into the cafeteria. There was no electricity or backup generator to light any inside part. After our harrowing experience trying to flee the hospital, we were scared, tired, hungry, and thirsty.

As we grabbed food, water, and soda to try to feed those of us who made it back safely, we decided it would be much easier to grab the carts of chips and dry food and bring it out to the front of the hospital, where others could more easily grab it as well. Karen and I made our way to the hospital's basement to see if there was damage to the lower part of the hospital. My office was in the basement, and I wanted to ensure it was still in good shape. The maintenance area was in the basement as well, and we were told by others coming back that there might be masks and regular flashlights with the maintenance staff. We were in emergency mode, looking for anything we thought we would need to care for ourselves and anyone else who showed up at the hospital again.

While going downstairs, Karen and I had to find a bathroom. It was pitch black in the basement of the hospital, and we continued using our cell phone flashlights to be able to find our way in the dark. As one might imagine, after going through such a harrowing experience for the last hour and a half to two hours, one might need to relieve oneself. There was no electricity, not even a backup generator, and there was also no running water. We were down to thinking about our basic needs and were still trying to decrease the anxiety of the last two hours that we did not even consider separating from each other. We figured there was safety in numbers, so we found a bathroom and did our business. There was no embarrassment or modesty under such circumstances.

We then entered the maintenance manager's office, where some others were, and sat down to rest, eat, and drink. We each found an N-95 mask for when we went back outside. There were some fresh air tanks, not oxygen, but we inhaled some of the air to clear out some stale, smoky air from our lungs from the outside. While the air was not oxygen, it was fresh and much easier to breathe than the smoke we had been breathing.

After about forty-five minutes of rest, Karen said, "I'm going to go outside to the emergency staging and triage area in front of the ER and see if I can help with any people who were hurt or couldn't escape the fire area like us." I thought that was a great idea, and while I had been away from direct patient care for a little while, I could still take vital signs and help move equipment and anyone who might need help getting to the triage area. I told Karen, "Wait for me. I'm coming too." I left my purse in the basement with the maintenance workers because I did not want to carry it around while working. I donned my N-95 mask and grabbed a large battery-operated lantern, and my cell phone, and Karen and I headed upstairs.

As we gathered the equipment, we needed from inside the ER to take outside the hospital, a vanload of seniors pulled into the parking lot. We think the seniors lived in a board and care home when the fire happened. The driver of the board and care home van tried to get them all to safety but knew they could not make it out safely, so he decided the best thing to do would be to try to shelter in place at the hospital. They hoped their residents could get help while everyone waited for the fire to burn down or for us to be rescued.

I helped the other nurses and some police and EMTs help the seniors out of the van to sit in chairs in the parking lot. I also helped the nurses and EMTs take their vital signs. I noticed the seniors were shivering, and I was unsure if they were in shock or just cold because the wind was picking up again as the fire made its own wind. I ran into the ER, grabbed all the blankets I could find, took them outside, and handed them to anyone who looked like they needed one.

As I finished with one group of seniors, another group showed up, and they were just as cold or in shock as the first group. I took a wheelchair and went further into the hospital to the surgical unit's linen closet, grabbed as many blankets as possible, and brought those out for the patients now sitting outside the emergency room. As I started to go back into the hospital for another blanket run, I was stopped by a security guard who said I could not go back inside because the hospital was now on fire. I was flabbergasted because I needed to return to the basement and get my purse, which had my car keys, wallet, and ID. I was told, "You can't go back," and he would not let me pass. I said, "You don't understand my car keys are in my purse, and I won't be able to drive my car out of here without them." He still would not let me go back in to get my purse. My heart sank.

Next, the Cal Fire lead told all the staff at the hospital that the people and equipment had to be moved to a safer location because the hospital was now on fire. The Cal Fire team told us that the helipad would be the best place to move to because there was no brush around it to burn. So, we began moving people to the helipad, and then all the equipment like the crash carts, the IV poles, the food carts, the gurneys, the wheelchairs, the supply carts, the water and fire extinguishers, flashlights, and lanterns. Anything we had taken outside to the front of the hospital had to be taken to the helipad. We moved quickly to the helipad with people and equipment.

As we stood on the helipad taking inventory of everything, I thought we needed to get a list of everyone who was there in case something terrible happened. We all started writing down names. I stopped for a moment to watch my office go up in flames, and I had a little juice left in my cell phone, so I tried to call my husband to let him know I was still alive and that we were now evacuating to the hospital helipad. As I talked to him to let him know I was okay, my cell phone battery ran out, and my phone went dead. I didn't know how much my husband had heard before my cell phone battery died. The next thing I knew, I was talking to dead air. Before briefly talking to him, I took a quick video of the hospital burning.

CHAPTER 8

NO RESCUERS COMING

J ust as we were getting back to making our list, our Cal Fire lead let all of us doctors, nurses, EMTs, and police officers know that he had just found out that we were not able to be rescued. He told us the smoke and wind were too much for an aircraft to get to us safely, so we were alone. He said their command center told him that the fire had burned down enough that if we hurried, we might be able to get out by car caravan, but if so, we had to go now. He asked us if we wanted to try to leave or stay on the helipad. We all said, "en masse," "Let's get out of here." We had all had enough; this day was becoming one long day from hell, and we were done. So, we packed patients and anyone who needed a ride into vehicles and caravanned out down Pentz Road. I was in the lead car with one of the doctors in her Honda Pilot. The same Honda Pilot that Karen and I had been behind on Pearson Road before returning to the hospital. Karen, another nurse, Nicole, and two people sheltering with us were in the car.

As we drove down Pentz Road heading toward Highway 70, we were driving very slowly, and we all were shocked by the devastation we were seeing. There were power lines down in the road and fire embers burning in the road as well. The doctor driving the Honda Pilot suddenly stopped, and I said, "What is wrong? Why have you stopped?"

She replied, "I don't want to drive over the downed powerlines in case they are still alive." I said, "It's okay. They probably are not live wires at this point, and your tires will be fine going over them; they are rubber."

So, she started forward again. I had to try to get her to hurry up, though, because we were the lead car and had quite a caravan behind us. She was being careful with all of us in her car, but I just had to keep prodding her, saying, "Keep going. Don't stop. We have many cars behind us, and we all have to get out of here." So, she picked up the pace and kept moving. In her defense, the devastation was horrific. It looked like a war zone. It reminded me of the pictures of World War II and the aftereffects of Hiroshima and Nagasaki after the atomic bombs were dropped. There were burnt houses, churches, other buildings, and utility poles around us. Everything around us was either smoldering, smoking, or burning.

As we drove through the devastation, it was the strangest thing. We would see large burned-out homes burned to the ground along with the forest around them, and then we would see one house that was hardly touched. There seemed to be no rhyme or reason for why one house had not burned and the rest of the block did. It was all incredibly quiet and spooky. In the car, no one spoke, or we spoke very softly as if we were now on hallowed ground that demanded respect for all it had suffered.

We neared Highway 99 and were going to turn right to go toward Chico, but we were turned back by sheriff deputies on the highway telling us the fire had jumped the highway and was heading toward Chico. We were not out of the woods yet. So, we headed toward Oroville instead. Oroville is just downstream from the Oroville Dam, the tallest dam in the United States. All I could think of was, "Will this day ever end?"

After being turned back from trying to go to Chico, we went to the only other place within the area that we could go to that was safe to wait out the fire. Oroville is in Butte County, California's county seat, approximately seventeen miles southeast of Paradise and eight miles east of Chico, California. Its population in 2018 before the Camp Fire was 19,174. It has the Oroville Dam in it, one of the primary sources of water for Butte County and one of the sources used to put out the Camp Fire. Oroville is where we dropped off two of our patient passengers. They had family in Oroville and decided to try to check into the hotel there. They wanted to rest, shower, and get some food while trying to contact family. That was a bright idea because we did not realize that the hotels and motels filled up with all the displaced Camp Fire survivors that day.

The rest of us in that fantastic Honda Pilot that carried us to safety away from the fire decided we would go with our driver, Dr. McKlarty, who would meet up with her daughter at a friend's house where they would be staying in Oroville. The rest of us were hoping for a bathroom and something to drink while we waited to reach Enloe Hospital in Chico once the fire was no longer threatening the highway.

As we got to Dr. McKlarty's friend's home, we discovered they were moving in that day and did not have their furniture yet, but they were terrific and took us all in, gave us food and water, and let us all use their bathroom. Then, sensing we might be in shock and needed to rest, they wrapped us all in soft blankets and let us rest on their carpeted floor for a bit. They let us tell our story of the day so far and just listened and gave us hugs. I, for one, needed those hugs and that warm, comfortable blanket. The wind had been so strong; we were all cold and exhausted, and the blanket felt terrific.

Dr. McKlarty's friends were so genuinely kind, and they kept saying they weren't doing much for us, but they were. We needed to be cared for and allowed into a safe place to try to rest and regain some of our strength to continue our day that was far from over. While I do not remember their names, I will never forget their caring and kindness that day. I am sure they did not need four people dropping in on them while trying to move into a new home, let alone people escaping a disaster whom they had to care for. Moving is stressful enough, and our situation made it much harder, but you would not know it from how they all dropped everything to care for us that day.

Nichole was able to reach her sister, and her sister was so incredibly happy to hear from Nichole that she dropped everything and came to pick her up. She also picked Karen and me up to take us all to Enloe. Nichole's mother was working at Enloe as a nurse and could not get away, but she wanted to see Nichole and hold her, and my family was there, too, whom I needed to see and hold onto. Nichole's sister was so genuinely lovely and hugged not only Nichole but all of us, and I am convinced those hugs got us through that long, exhausting day. Hugs are especially important in a disaster. People say that hugs are not much, but let me tell you, from one who has been through a disaster and come out the other side, a hug goes a long way in helping with recovery. I am convinced that hugs begin the disaster recovery and healing process.

As we all piled into yet another SUV, we bid goodbye to our newly made friends and let them return to the business of moving into their new home, but we thanked everyone for their wonderful hospitality. We were back on the road again, still trying to get to Enloe Hospital in Chico. While driving to Chico, Nichole's sister let us know what had been happening around the area. We were trapped and away from any news sources that said that the fire was still burning out of control and that firefighters from all over the United States were helping to fight the fire. She said the population of Chico quadrupled because of the fire, and there was so much traffic that it was hard to get anywhere fast. The smoke was still thick in the air, and it was everywhere. I noticed that I was having a more challenging time breathing than I had been, and I was unsure if it was because I felt safe enough to notice or if I was having a more challenging time breathing because of asthma. I would need a breathing treatment or two when I got to Enloe. I stopped talking to conserve my breath. I also noticed it was becoming more difficult to catch my breath.

CHAPTER 9

LEAVING THE FIRE ZONE

I t took us about an hour and a half to get to Enloe, which would normally have taken forty-five minutes. With all the traffic and the roundabout way, we had to snake our way through town to get there, but we finally arrived at Enloe Hospital at five thirty in the evening. While on our way to the hospital, we found ourselves debriefing and talking about what we had been through and some of the things we were afraid we had lost. One of the saddest things I remember hearing was that Nichole told us she had three horses on her property but had not gotten another horse trailer yet that held all three horses. She explained that she had just gotten her third horse and planned to get the new horse trailer the following week. She was worried sick that her husband would have to make a horrible decision to let one of the horses out on its own to try to leave the fire area while trailering the other two. I could not wait for this day to end.

Nichole's sister pulled into the emergency room parking lot and let us all out of the car. She found a parking spot, which I thought was a miracle. I thought it was even more of a miracle once I went inside the hospital and saw how crowded it was. We had come into the back of the emergency department so Nichole could get to her mother working in the emergency room and tell her she was all right. I found my way to the lobby in the front of the hospital, hoping my family would be waiting for me there. Karen decided to stay with Nichole and her family, so I bid her goodbye. We had already traded phone numbers so we could connect later. We agreed to call each other the next day to check in, and Karen, Nichole, and I hugged each other goodbye and went our separate ways.

As I came around the corner into the lobby from the emergency room area, I looked around for my husband, mother, stepdaughter, or any of them. I spotted my husband, BJ, standing next to Mom, and the tears began to fall. I had kept it together until then, and I did not want to cry, but I could not help myself. I hugged my husband and then my mom. None of us wanted to let the other go; we were just so happy to be together finally. I asked my husband, "Where are Bridget and the kids? Are they all, okay?"

He replied, "Yes, they are all fine. Bridget is at one of the nursing homes here in Chico, and Bill is on his way to Chico from the East Bay Area, where he was working today. The kids, dog, and Bridget's mom are slowly driving into Chico on Highway 32. They should be here in an hour or two." I realized everyone was alive, well, and accounted for. We were so incredibly lucky and blessed. I was very thankful at that moment. God had not only answered my prayers to save me but also saved my entire family.

At that moment, I realized that I had been holding an emergency battery charger in my hand that I got from the hospital emergency supply in Paradise. I had hoped to use it to charge my cell phone so I could use it again to call my husband. I had been trying unsuccessfully since leaving Paradise Hospital to attach it to my phone. I was still trying to get that stupid emergency battery charger to attach and forgot I did not need it anymore when I saw my family in the lobby of Enloe. My mom asked me what I was doing. I explained to her what I was doing and that I had yet to be able to attach the emergency charger to my phone since the helipad. After a few minutes of her watching me trying to attach the silly thing to my phone, she finally grabbed my hand and said, "Honey, put it down. You do not need it anymore. It's okay. You can stop." I looked at her, finally realizing what I had been doing, and started laughing. I had not realized how fixated I had become on such a silly thing.

I, of course, had to go to the bathroom again, but my mom did not want to let me go out of sight. She was so thankful to see me alive again that she came with me. After, BJ, Mom, and I went to the hospital cafeteria for food. I realized I was more thirsty than hungry and only ate a few bites. I was having difficulty breathing again or still, and my chest felt tight. I decided I should be seen by a doctor sooner rather than later, so we went to the ER.

The emergency room was filled primarily with evacuees from the fire. No one knew where to go or what to do. We could not go home because no one even knew if we had a home to go to. Many of us did not have family in the area, so we had no one to stay with, and some of us, like me, were injured or needed to be checked out by a doctor before we could go anywhere else. I took a seat after checking in at the front desk. I told the clerk I did not have my health plan card or anything on me to show who I was, but that I was one of the nurses at Feather River Hospital, and I just got there from having to shelter in place on the helipad. I gave her my name, and she said, "You shouldn't have to pay for this. It was work-related, so it should be fine." I took a seat and waited to be called.

As BJ, Mom, and I waited for me to be seen, we watched increased numbers of people file into the emergency room. I could hear different stories from different people all around us. One couple behind us was an elderly couple, and the woman was getting increasingly anxious. BJ and I heard her ask her husband, "Honey, what are we going to do? Where are we going to go?" And her husband said, "Honey, anywhere we want to." BJ and I looked at each other and said, "Yep. That's so true." We smiled and held each other's hand and laughed. It was so true. At that point, we had no possessions or responsibilities and were utterly unencumbered. We had lost our home, possessions, car, and job, so we could go anywhere we wanted to at that point. Nothing was holding us in that place. It was a very strange and somehow freeing feeling.

My name was finally called, and I went to the triage area. I told the triage nurse my name and why I was there. She asked me if I had lost everything, and I said I was unsure, but we had. I told her the hospital was on fire when I left it and that I did not know if it would be okay. I explained that I was one of the last nurses to leave the hospital and was glad to get out of there with my life. I had not meant to, but I caused the nurses to start crying when I was taken into one of the rooms just from listening to my day's story. She said that several of their nurses who lost their homes in Paradise were working at Enloe today. This is precisely what doctors, nurses, and first responders signed up for when we chose this as our career. It's also what our families signed up for, by extension.

As I was ushered into an emergency room and given a gown to put on, I waited to be seen by a doctor. I was given oxygen and a gurney to lie down on. An IV was started in my arm, and more questions were asked about the fire and about where I was in the fire area.

The doctor eventually came in, and I told him my story about the fire, my asthma, and the fact that I had been working with a fever since I got up that morning. I told him I thought I had the flu. He said he would give me a couple of breathing treatments along with oxygen and take some blood to see if it was the flu. I got breathing treatments from the respiratory therapist, and then the doctor returned to say I did not have the flu, but my white blood cell count was high, and I was still running a fever. I told him I had pain in the lower left side of my abdomen and that I had a history of diverticulitis. I said that was why I thought I had the flu. Diverticulitis is an inflammation in the large intestine that many adults get as they age. If bad enough, diverticulitis can cause the intestine to abscess or the intestinal wall to rupture and cause peritonitis. The emergency room doctor thought I should have a CT scan to see if I did have diverticulitis and, if so, to ensure I didn't have an abscess or a rupture.

I was given IV fluids and sent to the radiology department for a CT scan. It didn't take long before the emergency room doctor returned to the room to tell me that I had diverticulitis. He gave me IV antibiotics and would also prescribe two oral antibiotics for the next two weeks. He said he was happy the diverticulitis had not ruptured but was inflamed.

After being discharged from the ER, I was given my antibiotics prescription to take to Walgreens, the only pharmacy still open in Chico. As we went inside, my mom said she would be getting some things we needed for the night, and I went to stand in line at the pharmacy with BJ. The line was long because anyone who had been to the ER to be evacuated from the fire or had evacuated without their medication needed to get more. Unfortunately, Walgreens was the only pharmacy open at that time of night.

Just as we were at the pharmacy window, the metal shield went down, and we could not figure out what was happening. The shield went up, and the pharmacist looked frantic as she told everyone in line that the fire was coming this way and that they were evacuating the pharmacy so no more prescriptions would be being filled tonight. BJ and I swore simultaneously and then went to grab Mom and get out of there. We spotted Mom with a half-full shopping cart and told her we had to leave now. She said, "Now? I have to pay for this." I said, "We have to go. The fire is headed toward Chico, and this pharmacy is being evacuated. We need to leave." We left as quickly as we could and didn't look back.

As we left the pharmacy, I noticed my mother was still in her slippers. She said she had to leave without her shoes because they had to evacuate quickly. None of us had coats on. We only had the clothes on our backs. My mom had her purse, and BJ had his wallet, but my purse was at the hospital and was burned up as far as I knew. We had our cell phones, which we were taking turns charging from the car charger, and BJ had managed to grab my laptop, his laptop, and our essential papers box, and that was it. We had no change of clothes, toothbrush, toothpaste, or hairbrush. And our clothes all smelled like smoke.

On the way out of town, we called Bridget to let her know what was going on, and she said they were safe at a friend's home with the boys, Bill, and the dog. She also said they were watching the news and keeping track of what was going on, and they were safe and were not leaving Chico unless they had to. I told her we were headed to Williams, California, to spend the night and that tomorrow we would head up to Dublin, California, to my aunt's house, my mom's sister's. I let Bridget know we would call them the next day. I also told Bridget to call us if they had to evacuate to let us know where they were going so, we could keep track of them and where they would be. Bridget agreed, and we said good night and that we would talk in the morning.

IN SHOCK

CHAPTER 10

FIVE HOURS LATER

On our way to Williams, California (72 miles from Paradise), to the motel where I made a reservation at before leaving the ER, we were taking stock of what we had and would need in the morning. We were tired and wanted to get to where we were going and go to sleep. It had been a long day for all of us.

We drove over an overpass headed out of Orland, California, and I glanced to my right out the passenger side window and saw a bald eagle flying parallel to our car. I looked at it and noticed it was looking at us, and then I realized it was one I thought I recognized and that I had seen around Lake Paradise a few months before. It must have recognized my husband and me, too, because it let out a screech as if to say, "So long and take care; hope to see you again sometime." Then, the eagle flew away from us as if it was also going to find shelter for the night.

All of us in the car began to think about all the animals displaced or possibly even killed by the fire. We were reminded of the quail we used to watch on our street, the mountain lion, the bears, the squirrels, and all the other animals we had seen in the last four months in Paradise and Magalia. I was worried about what had become of them all and was wondering if they had gotten away from the fire. I thought about the deer I had seen at the back of our property and the buck I met in the parking lot of the hospital one evening after work. I thought about the silly little squirrel who adopted us as his pet humans and the family of skunks I saw one night coming home from work, the momma skunk, and her three little ones. I worried about those needing medical attention and how they would find food and clean water to drink. I also worried about all the pets who had been displaced and who ran away when their owners were trying to evacuate with them. I worried about all my friends and their families and wondered how many made it out and how many didn't. I worried about the elderly who could not move quickly or who needed help leaving their homes. I knew at that moment that not all the citizens of our town survived that day, but I did not know how many or who they were.

As we continued down the highway, I noticed how many "No Vacancy" signs lit up at each hotel and motel we passed along the way. I knew no rooms were available in Chico and Oroville because I had already tried those areas while making my reservation for my family. Still, I hadn't realized the lack of vacancies stretched so far south.

All I was thinking at this point was *thank God for credit cards and for BJ having his wallet with his credit cards in it*. I shuddered to think what people would do without a credit card to find a place to stay for the night. No shelters had been able to be set up yet, and the Red Cross hadn't shown up, and neither had any other agency to my knowledge. Everything happened so fast.

The churches in Chico were taking in as many people as possible, and Enloe Hospital was letting people stay in the lobby and ER waiting area. The churches only held so many people, and there were 56,000 people who were evacuated, displaced, and possibly homeless by the evening of November 8, 2018. The fire was still burning out of control, so no one could get back into Paradise or Magalia, and even parts of Chico were preparing to evacuate. The community was coming together for each other, though, and people were opening their homes and property to strangers to stay in spare rooms or on couches or for RVs to park and sleep inside for the night. Those of us who had credit cards and the means to do so were making our way out of the area to leave room for others who were unable to leave the area.

We finally arrived at our motel in Williams, California, and we noticed several people parked in the motel parking lot in their cars and trucks, just sitting around, not going anywhere, and not checking into the motel. As we exited the car to the motel, I told my husband, "Oh, I have a bad feeling about this." We walked into the lobby, waited our turn to check in, and were greeted with the news that the motel had been overbooked and no more rooms were available. I told the front desk clerk, "I confirmed a reservation a few hours ago." The clerk said, "I don't know what to tell you. We have no more rooms available." It was nearly midnight, and we were so tired we could hardly keep our eyes open. I knew it was no use making a complaint; there were so many other people in the same boat as we were, and they were deciding to camp out in their cars in the motel parking lot.

We looked at each other, piled back into our car, and continued down the highway. I immediately got on my cell phone and started to see if there were any other hotels or motels where we could find a room for the night or what was left of it anyway. We just needed a few hours of sleep, a hot shower, and some food, and then we could drive the rest of the way to my aunt and uncle's house in Dublin, California.

On the fourth or fifth try to find a motel, I found a Best Western Motel in Dixon, California, 106 miles away from Paradise, with two rooms available, so I booked them over the phone. Within forty-five minutes, we were pulling into the parking lot of the Best Western in Dixon. At this point, it was about 1:00 a.m. We checked into the motel and found our rooms. Mom took one room, and BJ and I took another. We said good night and would get together in the morning for breakfast.

BJ and I went into our room. We were so tired that we just put our stuff down and headed for bed. Then, I realized I had nothing to sleep in, but the clothes I had been wearing all day long smelled of smoke. BJ stripped off all his clothes because he didn't care. He slept in the nude anyway, but I could never do that. It's funny what things come up about yourself when you least expect it. I decided to strip off my blouse, pants, shoes, and socks and sleep in my underwear for the night. I so wanted to brush my teeth. It was cool, so we turned on the heat in the room and settled in for what was left of the night.

I slept for about an hour and a half when something woke me up. I forgot where I was; all I could tell was that it was dark, and I smelled smoke. I suddenly sat bolt upright in bed and was just about to wake up BJ to tell him to get out because I smelled smoke when I realized

I was smelling myself. I smelled like smoke. I started laughing hysterically and was afraid I would wake up BJ with my hysterical laughing, but I didn't. He slept through my fit of laughter at myself, and I laid back down and fell back to sleep. The longest day of my life so far was finally over.

CHAPTER 11

TWENTY-FOUR HOURS LATER

W e woke up later that morning, around 8 o'clock, to the sound of our phones ringing. Dazed and confused, we stumbled out of bed and answered our cell phones. Our good friends, our adopted family from Florida, called to ensure we were all still alive. They watched Paradise burn on the news the night before and could not reach us by phone. They were horrified and afraid we were all dead. BJ and I assured them we were all alive and doing okay but were in shock and were almost sure we had lost our house and my car and that I had come very close to dying in the fire. We told them we were away from Paradise, heading to my aunt's house in Dublin, California. We let Rich and Sandy know that Bridget, Bill, and our grandchildren may have also lost their home and that none of the towns in the fire area allowed anyone into the fire zone because the fire was still out of control. We told them our story and how we got out of the fire with nothing but the clothes on our backs, cell phones, laptops, and essential papers. We let them know nothing else could be retrieved out of the house before we all had to evacuate the area. We assured them we would keep in touch but needed to get dressed, check out of our hotel, and continue to my aunt's home.

Just as we were hanging up from our friends in Florida, BJ's sister Chris called from Maryland to ensure we were all still alive. Once again, we told her our story and assured her we were all alive and probably lost all our belongings, our home, one car, and my job. We assured her that Bridget and her family were alive as well and that they had more than likely lost their home, belongings, and one car, and they had also gotten out with only the clothes on their backs. We told Chris things could be replaced, but we could not replace people. We thanked Chris for checking on us and said we would let her know where we ended up, but for her not to worry about us. We also asked that she contact her other siblings for us and let them know we were all alive and would contact them once we got to a more permanent location. Chris agreed to call everyone for us and told us to stay connected, and we said we would.

Once the phone calls stopped, we decided to shower and go to the lobby for breakfast. Then we realized we had no brush or comb, no toothbrush or toothpaste, and no clean clothes to change into. We smelled like smoke, so we had to bathe at least, and we could call down to the front desk to see if they had any toothbrushes, toothpaste, and combs to use. We showered, dressed, and called the front desk to see what they could give us for toiletries to help us feel somewhat normal again. Luckily, they had combs, toothbrushes, and toothpaste that they sent to us in our rooms. We certainly did not look the best, but we felt cleaner and more alert. It is funny that we don't think about everything we need daily, like a toothbrush, toothpaste, a hairbrush, and clean clothes, until we don't have them anymore.

We filed into the breakfast area and were amazed to see toast, cereal, waffles, pancakes, eggs, sausage, bacon, juices, and good coffee. We were all in a state of shock, so it took us a moment to decide what to eat. I grabbed a table for us and waited until Mom and BJ got their breakfast to get mine. I felt so out of sorts. I felt as though I was walking around in a fog. I could not decide what to eat to save my life that morning. I kept thinking I just felt so out of it. I was still not feeling well from the diverticulitis and needed to find a drugstore to fill my antibiotic prescription, so I just figured that was what was wrong with me. It had not occurred to me that I might be in shock.

We paid our bill, checked out of the motel, and headed to the nearest bank branch to get some cash. After the bank, next on our agenda was going to the drug store to fill my antibiotic prescription and buy the toiletries, hygiene supplies, and everything else we needed. We needed everything. I don't think I've ever spent that much in a drugstore in my life. The drug stores had all been alerted to what had happened in Butte County with the Camp Fire, and they were all banning together to help us out. We got a good percentage off everything we bought.

Next, we needed to buy clothes, shoes, underwear, socks, pajamas, a robe, and a coat. It was getting cold, and we had no coats or sweaters. We stopped at some big box stores in Dublin, California. We needed inexpensive clothes and more than one or two items, so cheap seemed the way to go. Of course, the problem is that we are short, and none of us had an easy time buying clothes on a good day, let alone when we had nothing to wear after a fire. It was also late in the afternoon by the time we could do any clothes shopping, and we were all so tired we were not in the best spirits to shop anyway, let alone for everything from underwear to shoes.

We ended up settling for clothes that covered our bodies and not very well. We were either swimming in the clothes or just barely squeezing into them. We all left with a change of clothes, pajamas, shoes, socks, underwear, and a coat. It would do until we could find something better.

Again, we were surprised by how wonderful people can be when the chips are down, and a disaster happens in our United States. We were given percentages off on all our clothes, and everyone was so lovely and thoughtful. All the clerks were very understanding when we asked to keep the hangers, too. They said they just wanted some way to help and to please let them help us. They said they were so thankful for everything they had and wanted to help us because "But for the grace of God, it could be us." We were learning how important it was to allow others to help us. It was an extremely hard lesson that we were just beginning to understand.

CHAPTER 12

DUBLIN, CALIFORNIA

W e were exhausted and hungry when BJ, Mom, and I arrived at my Aunt Pat's and Uncle Raleigh's house in Dublin. Mom was going to stay with her sister for a while so BJ and I could take care of everything we needed, like the car insurance and homeowners' insurance, and requested a mortgage deferment and car payment loan deferment until the insurance could be settled. We were worried about Mom not managing the trauma of the fire and the loss of everything and wanted to minimize her stress level as much as possible. We thought that her staying with her sister, who she is close to, would be the best for her.

The three of us piled onto the front doorstep of my aunt and uncle's townhouse, looking like something the cat dragged in. My Aunt Pat and Uncle Raleigh greeted us at the door with hugs and smiles, happy we were all alive and safe. As we filed into their house one at a time, we got a hug and a kiss from each of them. When it was my turn, my aunt looked at me and said laughingly, "Don't take this the wrong way, honey, but you smell like smoke." I got an amazingly fast hug and a kiss, but

I understood because she was so right; I smelled like a campfire, no pun intended.

We came in and sat down and told our stories of where we were, what had happened to each of us the day before, and where we all were at various times throughout the day. Then, it was time for the news, and we all wanted to learn about what was happening with the fire. As we watched the news, they showed pictures of people fleeing the fire area and interviewed others. I recognized some of the people being interviewed as people who lived or worked in Paradise and others who had been with me at the hospital during the fire. It was nice to see people I knew who were doing all right. After a commercial break, the news showed pictures from the day before and the different roads in the town on fire. They showed people frantically fleeing the fire, and then they showed Pearson Road. It was an inferno with trees on both sides of the road going up in flames and cars backed up in stop-and-go traffic on that road.

I just lost it. I cried and cried and kept repeating, "That's the road I was on. That's what I was in. Everything was on fire all around me." You could have heard a pin drop in the room at that point. All eyes were on me, and there were shocked expressions all around. I didn't even care that I was falling apart, which is nothing like me. I usually don't cry in front of anyone except my husband, and only on rare occasions. I was bawling big, ugly tears, and I couldn't care less. I couldn't have stopped crying even if I wanted to at that point.

My aunt was the first to snap out of shock and grabbed and hugged me. Then she grabbed my husband, shoved him towards me, and said, "Here, hold your wife. She needs you." I just buried my head on BJ's shoulder and cried, not just the sniffly cry but the ugly bawling cry where your eyes are puffy, your nose is running, and you look like hell afterward. Before I knew what hit me, I was in a puddle on Aunt Pat's living room floor, my eyes red and puffy, wondering how I had survived, and I felt like I was suddenly back in my car on Pearson Road with fire and explosions all around. I could see the trees bursting into flames after being touched by embers, the propane tanks blowing up in the fire, and the gas tanks of burning cars exploding on the right and left of me.

All I can say is Post Traumatic Stress Disorder (PTSD) is a real thing, and it sneaks up on you when you least expect it. We were all walking around in a state of shock, and then suddenly, we were back in the trauma, reliving the nightmare all over again.

What I didn't realize until much later is that it is a normal state for trauma victims to be in. The first one to four weeks is a state of shock, and then suddenly, the shock wears off, and the actual post-traumatic stress disorder takes over.

After I could pull myself back together, BJ and I decided to head out to the motel I had booked for him and me for the night. My Aunt Pat and Uncle Raleigh's house is a small, cute little townhouse with one spare room. Mom would be okay in their spare room, but BJ and I would be too many bodies in their small space. I had already made a reservation at a motel with a kitchenette and pots, pans, and dishes anyway, so we could come and go as we needed to, and I figured that would work for us until we knew whether our house was really gone or not. At that point, we weren't sure. I think we were in a bit of denial, to be honest.

BJ and I had lived in San Ramon, just the next town from Dublin, for a year or two in the past, and I had worked there, too, and we still had several friends in the area. I had one of those friends contact me and ask if I was okay because she knew BJ and I had moved to Paradise, California, and she had been watching the fire on the news and was worried about us.

I let my friend Trisha know we were alive and doing okay but were afraid we may have lost our home and all our possessions in the fire. I told her we would be okay and that we had insurance, but we had little to no possessions now. Trisha immediately told my old bosses about the fire, and by the next day, BJ, Mom, and I were given clothes, suite cases, purses, shoes, socks, coats and sweatshirts, sweaters, cash, and gift cards. Everyone that I used to work with was chipping in to help us. We were so grateful to have anything. I couldn't believe their generosity. When you have nothing, anything is a blessing and so much appreciated. I can't even express how much that kindness meant to us that day. We were trying to be thankful for being alive, and we knew we had insurance that would kick in at some point, but we needed so many things all at once, like clothes, shoes, socks, underwear, and everything. We could not go shopping again immediately because we had to call insurance agencies for the house, car, and our possessions.

Thanks to our wonderful friends at Hill Physicians Medical Group, we didn't have to delay contacting insurance companies to go and buy everything we needed. As usual, leave it to nurse case managers to save the day. God bless case managers everywhere. We always know what is needed, how to get it, and when. Case managers are the unsung heroes of the healthcare world, but I might be a little biased about that since I am one.

Two days after the fire, it was my mother's turn to have a case of PTSD and shock occur. Mom woke up tired and worn out that morning but okay until she wasn't. Mom was outside on my aunt's deck helping my aunt sweep up some leaves when she collapsed. Aunt Pat called 911, and Mom was taken to the hospital to be evaluated.

Just after breakfast, BJ and I got a call letting us know Mom was going to the hospital in Pleasanton, one town away from Dublin. Aunt Pat said, "Your mom's okay, but she collapsed this morning and is going to the hospital. She was awake and talking by the time the ambulance got here."

BJ and I jumped in our car and immediately reached the Pleasanton Hospital. We got there so fast that we beat the ambulance there. I was the only one who could go into the room with Mom as soon as the doctor saw her, and I stayed there until the doctor decided what was wrong with her and why she collapsed.

The emergency room doctor thought she was suffering from a delayed stress reaction from everything we had been through. He gave Mom some medication to help her sleep and rest, and we took her out for lunch and then back to Aunt Pat's for some much-needed sleep. I was so thankful Mom was okay and had not had a stroke or a heart attack. We discovered much later that many of the elderly from Paradise, Magalia, and Concow, three of the main towns affected by the Camp Fire, had suffered strokes and heart attacks immediately after the fire related to stress; some of them died.

CHAPTER 13

DAY FOUR AFTER THE FIRE

On November 12, 2018, four days after leaving the fire and Butte County, BJ and I started making calls about our insurance. We had been through two other wildfires in California over the last two years and were educated on how to prepare. None of the other fires were nearly this bad, however. Unfortunately for us, we didn't heed all the education points given to us.

The other fires we had been in didn't spread as fast, and we had more time to plan our evacuation. I was a travel nurse in Carpentaria and Santa Barbara, California, for a thirteen-week assignment when the Thomas wildfire broke out. I was forced to evacuate from my apartment with as much as I could carry in my car because the smoke was so bad. I learned then the importance of leaving before being forced to evacuate will give you more time to plan your evacuation. When I finally evacuated, it was because of my asthma and the need to be away from the smoke in the air, not a mandated evacuation.

After the Thomas Fire and the Santa Rosa Napa Fire, BJ and I bought a metal file-carrying box with a lock on it. We put all our insurance papers, birth certificates, passports, retirement paperwork, credit card statements with numbers, tax receipts for the current and previous year, marriage certificates, and medical reports we could not easily replace in it. I also put my grandmother's high school yearbook in it as well. We put anything in that box that we did not think we could replace quickly enough, and we put it there in order to grab it as fast as we could in the event of a fire. We made a list of other things like photos, medication, and a few changes of clothes, jewelry, and family heirlooms that we thought we would at least be able to get out with the essentials.

Unfortunately for us and anyone else in the Camp Fire, there was no time except to be able to grab the essentials box. The Camp Fire was a whole different fire altogether than any other wildfire we had ever been through or even the Cal Fire firefighters had ever been through before. That fire left us less than four hours to evacuate before Paradise Ridge was engulfed.

My mom had my brother's cremains in a wooden urn in her apartment and did not have time to grab them. We notified the recovery crew with the cadaver dogs if they found human ashes on our property; they were the ashes from my deceased brother's cremains and not from a fire victim. My poor mother did not even have time to grab photos, and the only photo she had of her son was a tiny wallet-sized picture of Bill when he was eight years old. It was a school picture.

On November 13, 2018, our Paradise neighbors, whose mother's house was diagonally across from our home, called and texted us a picture of our houses and where they usually would have been. It wasn't a great picture, but it gave us an idea and some emotional preparation about our house that it was probably gone.

The official word did not come for another twenty-four hours. I was depressed and down and wanted to go home, but I realized we had no home to go to anymore.

We kept receiving gift cards from people to help us replace what we lost, but we all needed homes. We couldn't buy anything for our future homes because we had nowhere to put anything. People were trying hard to help, and we knew it, but we all needed places to live before we could replace what we lost. Fifty-two thousand people were displaced, and 18,000 buildings were destroyed. Where do you put fifty-two thousand people who have no place to live?

The insurance and mortgage companies would only agree to defer payments and only if we went to their offices to fill out paperwork requesting payment deferment. It was hell. The cable company, PG&E, and the water company could have also been more helpful to us after the fire. We had to ask them to stop billing us, or they would have continued charging us for their services that were no longer working.

We had to drive to Chico from San Ramon, California, two hours away, and go to the cable company to arrange for them to stop billing us for the equipment. At first, they were going to charge us for the destruction of their equipment in the fire. We had to insist on speaking to a manager about that ridiculousness. Luckily, the store manager waived any fees for us, but our daughter and her husband were not as fortunate. She spoke to the head of the cable company to finally get a resolution.

While we no longer owed anything on our mortgage, we owned an acre of burnt-out land in Paradise, California, that we still had to pay property taxes on to Butte County. We had to talk to the Butte Count

Clerk about how to pay our taxes and give them our new temporary address so they could bill us. Luckily, Butte County lowered the taxes to just what the land was worth in its current state instead of what our house and land would have been assessed for originally because we essentially owned a toxic waste plot of land in northern California that we couldn't rebuild on or live on in its current state.

Although our mortgage was deferred, the insurance company gave a third-party company $32,000.00, but the third-party company only gave us credit for $24,000.00. Our hotel costs were $150.00 a day at the San Ramon Marriott Residence Hotel. We had spent $3,200.00 so far and paid for it with our own credit card until our insurance would pay us back. Our insurance company needed to determine if our house was a total loss before they knew how much temporary housing allowance they would give us. We were concerned about finances at this point.

While having lost my job, my employer, Adventist Health, felt it was only right to continue to give all its Feather River Hospital employees a paycheck through February 5, 2019, to give us time to get back on our feet again. We were paid at the rate we were making at the time of the fire for an eight-hour day if we were full-time or part-time. Adventist Health also agreed to continue to pay our health, dental, and vision benefits until May 5, 2019, and they ended up extending that to the end of May. The Adventist Health leadership believed at the time that it was the right thing to do, and my family and I were and are incredibly grateful to them for that.

Another miracle happened throughout this back and forth with insurance, mortgage, taxes, etc. During the first of many Zoom meetings held by Adventist Health, I learned that someone had found and saved my purse from the fire. At the end of the meeting, my name was called out, saying that someone had found my purse before it was burned in the hospital basement.

All I can say is thank you to the wonderful person who turned in my purse entirely intact, with everything, including my money, still inside. I so desperately needed that news. Finding my purse complete and not gone gave me such a lift of spirit; it was another reminder of God's love and caring. He even saved my purse. Nothing was too small for God to take care of for me.

CHAPTER 14

THANKSGIVING 2018

T wo weeks after the Camp Fire started, it was still burning. Even though we were two hours away from the fire area, the smoke was still thick all over California and into Nevada. Thanksgiving Day came, and it was a much different Thanksgiving than I was expecting to have that year.

Aunt Pat and Uncle Raleigh had planned to visit Uncle Raleigh's side of the family out of state for Thanksgiving and could not change plans at that late date, so they left for Utah as planned. Mom, BJ, and I were going to buy a pre-made Thanksgiving meal from Nob Hill and heat it in Aunt Pat's microwave. Bridget, Bill, and our grandsons stayed in Chico and had Thanksgiving with friends. It was not exactly the happy family dinner I had imagined all year, with everyone around my big new dinner table. Oh well, we were all alive and relatively healthy. We had quite a bit to be thankful for anyway.

While we tried to make the best of things, I don't think we felt much like being around anyone. None of us wanted to bring down any of our friends, so we opted to be alone instead. We, of course, did the usual Thanksgiving thing of going around the table and saying what we were thankful for and how things could have been much worse. We could have saved time going around the table by saying dido after the first person said she was thankful for surviving the fire and having all our family safe and well because we all said the same thing.

Paradise was back on the news that Thanksgiving Day, as the reporters talked to the people gathered around a communal table eating a Thanksgiving dinner prepared by a gourmet chef. We were at Aunt Pat and Uncle Raleigh's house but were toasting our fellow Camp Fire survivors as we watched the news reports. They all looked about like we did. They were trying to be upbeat and thankful and, at the same time, feeling awful inside. God, forbid we show anyone around us how awful we feel; it was what all the reporters were waiting for. They were waiting for any of us to break down and start crying, but we are much stronger than I think anyone gave us credit for. We all made the best of a bad situation, enjoyed the food, and continued playing the hand we were dealt. On the bright side, at least no one had to cook.

After dinner, we cleaned up the dishes and said goodnight to Mom, and BJ and I returned to our hotel. We were all tired and not feeling much like doing anything. Besides, we were full of turkey and feeling mighty sleepy. BJ isn't much of a sports fan, and neither am I, so we got ready and went to bed a bit early. Bridget, Bill, and our grandsons Billy and Mark were coming down to San Ramon the next day, and we wanted to be well-rested and in good spirits when they got there, so an early night sounded good.

We couldn't wait to see Bridget, Bill, Mark, Billy, and their dog Pepper. We had not seen them for two weeks, and even though we talked with them every day, it was not the same as being able to hug them and laugh with them as before the fire when we could drop by to see each other at a moment's notice.

None of us are Black Friday shoppers; even if we were, we had nowhere to store anything we might buy anyway. We hoped to share what we learned about what was happening with the fire and any help the fire survivors were getting. Bridget, Bill, and the boys were living in Chico with one of Bill's work friends, and they were able to fill us in on the latest Camp Fire survivor news.

We learned from Bridget and Bill that the main post office in Chico had been saving mail for all of Paradise and Magalia, and we could go up there to pick it up at any time. This was good news because we had yet to determine when or if any of our mail would ever be delivered to us. We were not sure if the Paradise or Magalia post offices even survived the fire, let alone how we would get our mail now.

I spoke with Bridget, and she and I both had been feeling the effects of post-traumatic stress disorder. Neither Bridget nor I had been getting more than three or four hours of sleep a night, and we had nightmares we couldn't remember after waking up, but our spouses let us know we must have been having nightmares or night terrors because we were crying out in our sleep. We both felt so tired and listless and had no energy to do everything we needed to do.

Bridget had no job but was getting a lot of e-mails and messages about applying for jobs as a certified nursing assistant (CNA) with other skilled nursing facilities (SNFs) in the Chico area. Bill was still working, so she was not feeling too stressed to get another job immediately. I was good, too, but I wanted to nail something down before February 5.

I was still finishing my diverticulitis antibiotics and feeling some lasting GI effects. I could not keep to as bland a diet as I wanted because I could not cook how I was used to and eat however I needed to. We were planning a trip to Chico to visit the post office and the Disaster Relief Center we heard about from Bridget and Bill. The old Sears in the Chico shopping mall has become a Disaster Relief Center. It has many different tables and booths with everything the Camp Fire survivors might need, so we planned to go up there one day the next week.

We were still not allowed into the fire area because the fire area was still too dangerous with falling trees and toxic waste, so we weren't going to be able to see our houses. We wanted to see our property to see what, if anything, survived. We were also anxious to get together with other survivors and talk with friends to ensure they were doing okay, too.

Bridget, Bill, the boys, and Pepper decided to stay at our hotel and visit another day. One day just was not enough after the hell we had been through. We enjoyed trading stories about what we had been up to the last two weeks with insurance and all the other nonsense we'd been dealing with. Bridget, BJ, and I had to make the same calls to the utility companies and the cable and garbage companies, and it was just nuts to have to do that, in my opinion. It's not like the whole town didn't have a stop date on all utilities or anything. Everything stopped on November 8, 2018. Some things we found were just too crazy for words. I kept wondering where everyone's common sense went to.

CHAPTER 15

TWO WEEKS AFTER THE FIRE

Two weeks after the fire, there were 130 people still missing from Paradise, Magalia, and Concow. Fifty-two thousand people were without a home, and 58 people were known to be dead. Countless pets were missing, and at least seven or more homeless shelters were filled with Camp Fire survivors living in them. To my knowledge, neither FEMA (Federal Emergency Management Agency) nor the Red Cross was involved with the shelters at this point. There were evacuation shelters in the Fair Grounds and various churches from the Chico and Oroville areas. They were being staffed by volunteers, nurses, social workers, and anyone else who wanted to help. The National Guard were on their way, and so were the Red Cross and FEMA. FEMA sent water and were bringing trailers for people to live in when they came. Airbnb opened as many places as possible for free for Camp Fire survivors.

It had been two weeks since the day of the fire, and we were still living in a motel or hotel. I am never sure what the difference is between the two. Our small room at the Marriott was okay, but it was a little small. We had a little kitchenette and pots, pans, and dishes, so we could at least cook some things on top of a stove or microwave; we were in one room, like a studio apartment. A studio apartment is suitable for a vacation for a week or so, but after that, it gets old. It was warm and had everything we needed, and we even got some socialization during the week during happy hour in the lobby. Doing laundry was a pain in the bottom, however. There was only one laundry room with four washers and four dryers for the entire Marriott complex, and each load cost $1.50 per wash and $2.00 to dry each load. The machines only took quarters. We went to the bank to get change a lot.

We drove up to Chico early Monday morning on November 26, 2018, to give us time to get what we needed to do done and get to my friend Holly's house early enough to spend some time catching up with her. Holly was a friend I worked with at Feather River, and she graciously opened her house and bedroom for BJ and me whenever we needed to get our mail and visit the Disaster Relief Center. Holly was also one of the nurses volunteering at some of the shelters, both for people and the shelters for animals. Two of the shelters were opened to found animals that had run away during the fire and pets that were being held for some people in the shelters.

We made it to the main Chico Post Office, which was in the middle of downtown Chico, around 11 a.m. The traffic was horrendous, and finding a parking space took much longer than we thought. We did not realize how having 52,000 people displaced from Paradise and Magalia and the surrounding small towns would have affected the town of Chico. It was overcrowded, and the homeless population increased exponentially. People were sleeping in parks, doorways, and wherever they could find places to sleep out of the elements. When we finally reached the post office, the line to pick up mail was around the block.

BJ and I got in line and waited with everyone else who was there to pick up their mail. Some people knew each other and were hugging and finding out where each other was now. Others like us stood quietly, trying to make the best of a difficult situation. Everyone was polite and kind to each other. We struck up light conversations with people around us to pass the time while in line, and I noticed how most of us in line were wearing what looked like hand-me-down clothes and clothes that were not exactly appropriate for the changing weather. People were like us, wearing clothes that were second-hand, and really, we all looked like a whole group of homeless or refugees camped out at the post office. When I thought about it, I realized we were homeless and refugees, probably all wearing clothes from friends, family, or thrift stores.

I began to listen to the conversations around me, and I realized we were all trying to get by the best we could, and most of us were not nearly as adept at getting by as many of the longer-term homeless population were. They could have taught us a thing or two, I'm sure. At that moment, I finally began to feel like a refugee from a war zone rather than a wildfire disaster survivor.

When we finally made it up to the front door of the post office, we were shuttled from one area to the other, and we were told to fill out cards with our old address and then our forwarding address on it and all the names of the people who lived in our old address before the fire. We waited patiently for our turn at the post office windows to pick up our mail. BJ and I had planned to ask about getting a post office box. Before we got up to the window to ask one of the postal attendants about a post office box, the post office attendants were going around telling everyone there were no more P.O. boxes available.

It started getting dark, and we were still not up to the post office window. BJ and I were two of a handful of people still waiting for our mail to be found. Finally, at six o'clock, just as the post office was supposed to close, we were told that the bag of mail with our mail in it was never brought into the post office but instead was locked in one of the mail trucks at the other post office until tomorrow. We would have to return the next day and stand in line again. We were tired and hungry and felt like victims who depended on strangers' kindnesses for almost everything. I hadn't felt like a victim until that day.

We made our way back to my friend's house feeling tired and defeated, and like the ugly stepchildren no one wanted to look at or be around because we were the cause of all the new problems plaguing their town. We had gone from survivor to victim and were being blamed for all the new problems in Chico. Shame and blame the victim time. How soon we were forgotten. I wondered what happened to "but for the grace of God, go I?"

Even the president of the United States, Donald Trump, didn't know who we were. He kept calling our town Pleasure, California, not Paradise, California. President Donald Trump also blamed us, the Camp Fire victims, for the fire. He said the fire was all our fault because we did not rake our forests, whatever that means. He insisted that we hadn't been maintaining our forests, and that's why the fire happened. Much of the forests around Paradise and Magalia are federal forest lands that are supposed to be maintained by the federal government. It is illegal to do anything with a federal forest without the federal government's permission. Only trees on private property could be maintained, and we needed permission to cut down any of our trees, and only if they were deemed sick or dead were we able to have them cut down. If we had them cut down, if they were healthy, we would have to plant new trees of the same type in their place according to the town ordinances. As far as my husband and I knew, none of our 200-foot sugar pine trees were sick or dead before the fire.

RECOVERY

CHAPTER 16

RECOVERING PHYSICALLY

After we were let back into the fire area to see our property, the question then was, what do we do now? BJ and I were at a loss for what to do and where we wanted to go. We knew we couldn't live in the hotel for too much longer, but I wanted to take some time to figure out what we wanted to do next. Do we rebuild right away, or do we wait to rebuild? The problem was that we were running out of money for housing. The hotel was too expensive to keep living there, and I felt I needed to have more security. That meant I needed to find a new job as soon as possible and someplace to live.

I remembered my nursing training about Maslow's hierarchy of needs. Maslow said that we all have a hierarchy of needs that we must fulfill one after the other, and we cannot move to the next level of needs until we fulfill the needs before it. He said we have first physical needs, then safety and security needs, then love and belonging needs, then self-esteem needs, and, finally, self-actualization needs. Thinking about these needs, I realized I needed to feel secure. We had our physical needs met for the moment, and we had a roof over our heads and food in our stomachs, and we were healing from our trauma. What we were missing was a feeling of security and safety.

BJ and I talked about what we were feeling, and I told him that I needed to feel secure, and living in a hotel was not giving me that. I said I wanted to feel safe and secure, and to me, that meant I needed to find a more permanent place to live. I needed a home and not just a place to live. He heard what I was saying, so we both started to think about what we wanted to do about our next home. We thought about whether we wanted to rent a home, whether we wanted to rebuild our home, and, if so, what type of home. We knew that we would have to clear our land of all the toxic debris before we could rebuild. We also knew that would take a while because of the sheer volume of property that needed clearing. We also were aware that there were not enough builders for the number of homes needing rebuilding. Even if we began rebuilding immediately, we would not have a home to live in for at least a year. So, we decided to look for a place to rent for the time being. The next question was, where do we live? Technically, we could live anywhere we wanted to where I could find work. I'm a nurse; that didn't narrow it down.

We both wanted to be as near to our daughter, son-in-law, and grandchildren as possible, but we also needed to be in an area where I could find a nursing job doing the type of nursing I wanted, if possible, and that was case management. We decided to start trying to find someplace to live as close to Paradise and Chico as possible. I hoped Adventist Health would rebuild the hospital soon so I could work again at Feather River within a year or two.

However, as luck would have it, there were no rental properties and very few properties for sale anywhere near Paradise, California. The available properties had multiple offers, and we were not willing to pay a considerable amount to rent or buy a property while planning to rebuild our home. That left us trying to get a place to rent as close to Paradise as possible in an area we could afford, where I could find work as a nurse case manager.

During one of our trips to Chico, while staying with our friend Holly, she told us about some other friends of hers who were burned out of Paradise in the Camp Fire, too, and they relocated to Auburn, California. She said it is a small town in the Sierra foothills, and her friends said it was quite a charming little town. Sacramento is only forty-five minutes to an hour away, so if I couldn't find work in Auburn, I could find a job nearby. So, BJ and I started looking online for rental properties in Auburn and planned to see the houses as soon as possible. We were looking for a three-to-four-bedroom house with a mother-in-law suite or guest house on the property. We were not planning on being too fussy, though, and would settle for a house that had a split floor plan with the master bedroom either on a different floor or on the opposite side of the house on the same floor. The plan was for Mom to continue to live with us wherever we ended up living. Auburn was only two hours away from Chico and Paradise, so we could still visit the kids relatively easily, and they could visit us as well.

BJ and I had already decided we could not afford to move back to the East Bay area of California even if we had wanted to move back there because the housing prices had skyrocketed. We couldn't afford high rent if we planned to rebuild our house in Paradise. We looked at houses in Benicia, where we lived before moving to Paradise, and the housing prices were soaring way over what we were willing to spend. Our estimate for the top amount we could afford to spend on rent was $2,400 monthly. We were hoping to spend under that amount, but we were realistic because the rental prices had also increased, so we decided to spend up to that amount monthly on rent.

We looked at several houses for rent in Auburn, California. We hadn't rented a house for several years because we had owned our own home, and of course, we needed background checks and credit checks before anyone would seriously consider renting to us. We were also shocked at what type of home our $2,400 would get us. We were unwilling to rent an apartment because we felt we would need more extensive square footage to allow for the privacy we would need between BJ and me and my mother. The type of property we were looking for was preferably a single-family home or townhome. The houses we were looking at were unacceptable to us because they were either too small or not to a standard, we were willing to live in.

Finally, we saw two houses we might consider and chose a three-bedroom, two-bathroom single-family house with a den. The house was in a noticeably quiet area of South Auburn on Sawka Drive. The house was about 2,400 square feet and had a two-car garage with a lovely garden for a backyard. We were incredibly happy to find this home and decided it would suit us nicely. We put a down payment on it and began the background and credit checks process.

Once we got the keys to the new rental home in Auburn, it was time to go shopping for furniture and everything else needed for a home. We would need bedroom furniture, living room furniture, dishes, a dining room table, chairs, glassware, etc. Thinking about shopping for furniture for our house was an exciting proposition until it wasn't. It became difficult when we realized we could not get any used furniture to our house without a truck. We had about $131,000 to replace our personal property and figured we would purchase everything new. Then, when we walked into a furniture store to buy new furniture that could be delivered to our house, we realized we didn't know where to start because we needed everything. We walked into the store and stopped dead, not knowing which way to go first. Luckily, the furniture store manager helped several families rebuild their homes after the Santa Rosa Napa Fire, so she knew how to help us.

One thing I appreciated from the sales associate was her understanding and experience. She took us room by room, and we purchased everything we would need furniture-wise and accessories like dishes, placemats, napkins, bed sheets, and pillows. Our pots, pans, towels, and blankets had to be found in a different store, but everything else we could get in this one store. It was an exceedingly long shopping day but well worth it. Finding styles, we liked was difficult because the furniture we had before the fire was bought over time piece by piece. We had time to be picky and choose pieces we liked that fit our taste. After the fire, we had to take what we could get for the significant pieces of furniture and then go from there. Unfortunately, furniture styles had changed and were not always to our liking. We spent about $40,000 in one day. We still needed to bring Mom shopping for her replacement furniture, but that was for another day. We were dead tired by the end of the day. The reality of replacing everything was just exhausting.

The next day, BJ and I took Mom shopping for her replacement furniture, and she was also overwhelmed. At first, she didn't understand that BJ and I were paying for all her replacement furniture. She thought she would have to pay for her replacement furniture out of pocket. I told her it came from our insurance money because she was with our family. I think Mom was still a little shell-shocked from the fire. Once she realized the insurance was paying for her replacement furniture, she was much more willing to pick out nice furniture she liked. We spent another $20,000 for her replacement furniture the next day, and then we had to decide when to deliver the furniture. We had to time the furniture delivery as close to our move-in day as possible because we needed a bed and furniture to sit on before moving into the new rental house.

Many of the renters from Paradise and Magalia who lost all their individual property in the fire didn't have any renter's insurance. The property owners of the rental properties were not required to replace their renter's belongings, so many didn't. Many of the homeowners didn't have insurance for the replacement of their own belongings, let alone their renters. It was exceedingly difficult for the renters who were now homeless to save money for another rental down payment and monthly rent and be able to afford even secondhand furniture, and that's why several months after the fire was out, many of the Paradise and Magalia residents were still living in shelters.

We moved into our new rental on December 12, 2018. As it turned out, we were all moved in, but not all our furniture could be delivered until well after Christmas. The bedroom set and living room couch sleeper sofa we wanted were on backorder. We didn't get all our furniture delivered until February 2019. Furniture stores today don't overstock like they used to in the past with furniture. The stores only have a few items in stock and order the rest as needed. If the furniture can't be ordered from another store, the purchaser must wait until a new shipment has been made and delivered.

Christmas wasn't much easier than Thanksgiving was in 2018. We all needed so much, and being able to get out to shop was difficult with only one car. Mom did not drive, so she was trying to order everything online and get everything delivered on time for Christmas. None of us wanted to get a Christmas tree or even decorate for Christmas, let alone shop for Christmas, so we didn't get a tree or put-up decorations. We would have had to buy a tree and all the new decorations, and we couldn't do it. We gave out many gift cards that year because the kids didn't have any place to store things, and gift cards were easier to mail.

I was still not working by the time Christmas came. I had not found another job yet, so money was tight. We had the insurance money but did not know when I could find another job or if I could find one doing what I wanted, so we were hesitant to spend it. I was 57 years old and living in Auburn, California, where the nursing wages were much less unless you were willing to work in the hospital. I had been working three days a week with benefits at Feather River Hospital and was looking for a similar position. Unfortunately, there were no inpatient hospital case management jobs that were part-time benefited positions. Most of the benefited positions for case management were full-time only. I could work per diam, but then I would have to buy my medical, dental, and vision benefits. The outside hospital case management positions paid much less than in the hospital, and they were full-time if I wanted any benefits. Also, no one seemed to want to hire new employees around the holidays.

CHAPTER 17

FINANCIAL RECOVERY

February 5 came around much faster than I was ready for, and I still needed and had not found a new job. I had been looking quite steadily for one since December. I cannot remember how many resumes I filled out and sent into different nursing jobs. I even went to one of the other Adventist Health hospitals to interview and tour the hospital to see if I could work there as a case manager. It was two hours away from Auburn, California, and was just too long of a commute for me, so I turned that position down. I could not fathom commuting two hours one way to work and two hours home every day. The position was full-time, and I could not commute those five days a week. We liked Auburn and did not want to move again, so I kept looking.

At the end of January or first of February, we learned that the fire was started by faulty PG&E equipment and was one of about 1,500 fires for which PG&E had been responsible between 2017 and 2018. At this same time, a law firm approached us about being part of a lawsuit against PG&E. The firm we spoke with and decided to go with was a firm with several different attorneys working together to file individual claims against PG&E for the fire victims. It was explained to us by the attorneys that PG&E had been responsible for at least 1,500 other fires throughout California and that the Camp Fire was the most destructive. By this time, the Camp Fire was known to have killed 85 people, destroyed over 153,000 acres, and destroyed 18,000 buildings, most of them homes; it had displaced 52,000 people, and the town of Paradise, California, was destroyed. Paradise and parts of Magalia and Concow looked like war zones. They looked like Hiroshima and Nagasaki after the atomic bombs were dropped. We were angry and grieving. We had lost our home, livelihood, and car, and I nearly died in this fire. I was not working; I had no prospects yet, and we needed to be made whole. So, we filed our lawsuit against PG&E.

I finally broke down and filled out paperwork with unemployment when February 5 came and went, and I still had no job. The unemployment department insisted on increased paperwork to be filled out before considering giving me any money. It became clear that finding a job was the only way I could get help. I felt desperate and unwanted as a nurse by anyone, even though I had 36 years of nursing experience in hospital, long-term care, hospice, home care, and case management. I had management experience and had been a director of three different hospices. I couldn't figure out why I wasn't getting offered a job. I had gone to several interviews, and when I finally heard back from the different potential employers, they had said something to the effect that they had decided to go in a different direction or they hired a different candidate. I kept sending out my resume and applying to many different nursing positions, and still nothing. I was beginning to feel I was not being hired because of my age. I couldn't think of what else it could be.

I discovered I was not the only person having trouble finding work from the other employees from the Feather River Hospital in Paradise. Many of the older nurses and social workers looking for work were also having difficulty finding a job. I wondered if there were so many people from Paradise, Magalia, and Concow looking for work in northern California that the different employers could afford to be picky.

I then decided that if I could not find a permanent job, maybe I should consider a temporary one. I started filling out applications with temporary nursing employment agencies. We were dipping into our home-building savings to pay our rent. I was at an incredibly low point. I was depressed and feeling hopeless to the point of considering suicide. I was not thinking clearly at all. I was also not sleeping well and had flashbacks about the fire daily.

Toward the end of February, I was finally given a temporary job as a case manager for an insurance company that managed Medi-Cal insurance. I had been making $56.00 an hour working three days a week at Feather River as a hospital case manager, but outside the hospital, all I could get was a job paying less than $48.00 an hour, and I had to work five days a week. The job was in Sacramento, so I also had to drive an hour each way to the job and back home to Auburn. I was desperate to be working, so I took the job. If the company liked me after ninety days, they could hire me full-time away from the temporary agency, and then I would get benefits.

Luckily, Adventist Health covered my medical, dental, and vision benefits until May 2019, so at least I had benefits until I could earn my benefits at my new job. I was not looking forward to my long commute of 45 minutes to one hour, but I needed to do what I could to take care of my family's financial security. I was unsure if I was ready to return to work, but I knew we needed to pay our rent and save money to rebuild our home in Paradise.

Unfortunately, as of the writing of this book, we still have not rebuilt our home in Paradise, mainly because we see no reason to rebuild a home that will burn down again in a new wildfire, and our insurance settlement wouldn't have afforded us to build a home built out of materials that will not burn down. I don't believe rebuilding a home that will burn down again in another wildfire makes any sense. We also can no longer afford the necessary fire insurance to own a home near a forest. As it stands right now, we may end up paying most of our settlement money to the Internal Revenue Services. It used to be that we could deduct attorney fees from our federal taxes, but since the Trump presidency, that deduction was removed.

While Republican representative Dug LaMalfa and other Democratic representatives on both sides of the aisle are trying to rewrite the law so that disaster settlements are no longer taxable, as of today, they still are for federal and some states.

CHAPTER 18

EMOTIONAL RECOVERY

I began my new job on March 1, 2019. Driving to and from Sacramento's Natomas area was quite harrowing. The traffic on Highway 80 was nothing I was used to. The East Bay area had traffic, too, but it was primarily stop-and-go. The traffic on Highway 80 was speeding over 70 to 80 miles an hour in and out of lanes. I was exhausted when I got to work or home from work. I liked the job and the people I was working with, though. They were so genuinely nice, and everyone was helpful to me. I cannot remember how often I told my story about escaping the Camp Fire. On the one hand, that was hard to do; on the other hand, it was helpful for me to talk about the fire. It was very strange. One day, while walking through the parking lot to get lunch at the café, I saw a car that reminded me of my Chevy Volt. I started to cry, remembering how that car had been burnt and destroyed after I tried to make my escape down Pearson Road during the fire.

Any little thing could bring tears to my eyes. I found myself feeling stressed all the time, and any small thing could make me angry. My emotions were everywhere, and I did not know why. We had a lovely home, and I was making okay money, but I felt like I was holding on by a thin little thread. I felt like any minute, I was going to fall apart and have a nervous breakdown or something. That's when I realized I needed to get some help.

I am a nurse, so I, of course, knew about post-traumatic stress disorder or PTSD. Still, I didn't know that all other stresses that a person has gone through in his or her life can cause a PTSD situation to be made worse because the trauma suffered from the event is compounded by all the other stressful events a person has already suffered before the actual traumatic event. This final event is essentially the straw that breaks the camel's back.

PTSD is a condition that affects many people after a traumatic event. There are two phases to this condition. The first is acute stress disorder, usually lasting up to one month following a traumatic event. This acute stress disorder has symptoms of numbness in your feelings, reliving traumatic events through memories or dreams, and avoiding anything that could remind a person of the traumatic event. These symptoms can be so bad that they can prevent the person experiencing them from getting out of bed, let alone getting dressed, showering, or eating. Treating this acute stress disorder involves providing the affected person with a safe and calming environment. The affected person may need medication to help calm him or her if the trauma is very severe. Suppose a person going through this is so severely affected that he or she cannot function properly. In that case, this person may need someone to help them with fixing food, bathing, dressing, or keeping a calming environment.

The second phase of PTSD usually begins 30 days after the traumatic event and lasts the rest of the person's life, and people usually need counseling to learn to live with PTSD. Symptoms of PTSD are usually feeling upset by anything that reminds them of the traumatic event, having nightmares about the event, having vivid memories about the trauma, avoiding places that remind a person of the traumatic event, feeling bad about oneself or the condition of the world, having a feeling of numbness and a loss of interest in things the person used to care about, feeling anxious or jittery, and having difficulty sleeping or a lack of cognitive focus.[6]

After doing some research, I realized I needed counseling and the correct type of counseling from someone specializing in post-traumatic stress disorder. So, because I had been a nurse for quite some time, I knew some counselors specialized in helping people through traumatic events. I looked online to see if any counseling groups were helping with the Camp Fire victims counseling. I discovered that a group of psychologists nationwide are doing pro-bono work with the Camp Fire survivors—the Trauma Recovery EMDR Humanitarian Assistance Program. I searched and found counselors from the Trauma Recovery EMDR Humanitarian Assistance Program in my area of Auburn, California, and left messages asking if they had any availability. Two were available, so I chose the provider with the soonest available time on a Saturday or evening that I could get.

The counselor I found was a woman who practiced Eye Movement Desensitization Reprocessing, or EMDR Therapy. This therapy uses rapid eye movement to help the survivor tap into their feelings and emotions of the traumatic event and then experience those emotions as if they were still in the event. It seems strange, but if you have ever been reading a book and suddenly began feeling overwhelmed with emotions and did not understand what was happening to you, that is essentially EMDR at work.[7]

The latest techniques have incorporated beat-to-beat variability into the process, which seems to work more quickly than the original EMDR therapy. I am not exactly sure how it works, but I am proof that it does work. I could tap into the feelings I had been suppressing of the fire that I did not even realize I had been suppressing. I was in a safe environment with a professional therapist who helped me relive my experiences and feel my pain, fear, anger, and sadness as if it were happening right then so I could work through it. There is a saying, "The only way out is through." This is essentially how you begin dealing with PTSD.

I went to this therapist for several sessions until I felt calmer and able to understand and better cope with my feelings. I learned that PTSD would never go away completely but that having these feelings was okay and very natural. I also learned that when I have an episode of PTSD, either after a dream or after seeing something that reminds me of the fire and what I went through during the fire, I should allow myself to feel the feelings and be in the moment with those feelings and let them wash over me and get to the other side of them. Each time I do this, the feelings are less and less intense, and I can acknowledge them, and by doing that, they lose their power over me.

I continued with therapy for a while longer with another therapist to help me continue to work through some of the emotions that were coming up in talk therapy. Still, I seemed to need more explanation and talking about it to get it to a more manageable place, but then, of course, the pandemic happened. Everyone was no longer meeting in offices, and video counseling sessions had not been developed yet, so I had to stop therapy. I had gotten to where I felt I could manage my day-to-day life without melting down or feeling like I could not cope. My anxiety level was lower, and I did not feel like I wanted to bite people's heads off for no good reason anymore, so I felt I would be okay for a bit. I still have days when I remember the fire, and PTSD rears its head yet again, but that is just another piece of the trauma melting away. Eventually, I hope to get to a point where I notice a feeling and can tell myself, "Isn't that interesting?" With little to no emotion, I can go on with my day.

CHAPTER 19

WHAT IS NORMAL?

B J, Mom, and I had all been back to Paradise to our property by March of 2019, but as we already knew, not much survived the fire. We found a few things that had survived the fire and were surprised at what they were. One of the most astonishing things to BJ and me was the wooden sign his father had made for us with our last name burnt into it. It was a sign about 18 inches long by 3.5 inches wide with our last name, Rhatigan, burnt into it in cursive script. It was made of wood, for goodness' sake, and it was found on the ground where our front wooden fence had been. The fence had a tori gate at the entrance of it, and that tori gate was utterly gone, burnt away along with the rest of the fence, but our Rhatigan sign was just fine as if it had not been touched by the fire at all. It was found lying on the ground where the tori gate had been.

We also found a porcelain figurine that my great aunt Alice made many years ago when my mother was a young girl. Aunt Alice used to make porcelain figurines and fire them in her kiln. She hand-painted them and added lace and other things for embellishments. The lace was gone on this figurine of a 15th-century lady I got from Aunt Alice years ago in 1983. Aunt Alice gave it to me because, as a child, I used to play with it when I came to visit her. I was so relieved that this survived the fire. This figurine was the only thing I had to remind me of Aunt Alice because all pictures of her were burnt in the fire.

Other things that survived were equally strange to have lasted, like a syrup pitcher my mother had from when she was a little girl, an angel plant holder my brother gave my mother before he died, a clay race car planter my husband had that was given to him by his daughter for Father's Day when she was a little girl under seven years old. And a teacup from my teacup collection made from porcelain. Only one teacup survived, however. A small porcelain bud vase from when my mother was a little girl, some clam shells, and an abalone shell Bridget found when she was nine while beach combing with BJ and me in Pacific Grove, where we once lived. None of our picture albums survived, so we have no pictures of anything before the fire except what pictures were on our cell phones. Nothing else from our house survived. We were picking up the surviving pieces of our lives before the fire, and not much was left of our old lives.

My whole world had been turned upside down. I began to search for some semblance of normal. I was trying to regain some of my previous life before the fire. I had a job, a house, a car, clothes I loved, and people who were friends and a community. I was trying to return to a "normal life" again.

We investigated rebuilding our home in Paradise and realized that there needed to be more contractors or builders for everyone who lost a house in order to rebuild. It would take up to a year to get even a manufactured house or mobile home built on our property, which would cost us at least $250,000 to $300,000 to build. I never liked mobile homes and did not feel they would give us the type of equity we sought anyway. We decided to wait until we could find a contractor to rebuild our home, but we also did not want to rebuild the type of home that would be in danger of burning again should we have another wildfire in the area. BJ, Mom, and I decided we did not want to be one of the families who rebuild a home only to have it burn down again several years in the future because we built the same type of home that did not survive the first fire.

BJ and I investigated different types of homes that would be fireproof as much as possible. I noticed that anything we had made from steel, like our carport, horse trough planters, and garbage can, did not burn like the wood buildings did. We also considered building a stucco house because many stucco homes did not burn either. Then we looked at the cost of building those more fireproof types of buildings and realized it would cost us about $300 a square foot to build a stucco or metal house. Our insurance only gave us $160,000 for rebuilding our home. Our house was a 2,400 square-foot home, so, at $300 a square foot, our house would cost $720,000 to rebuild the same size home we lost. The house we lost cost us $399,000 to buy. We knew we could not afford to rebuild the same size house we lost. This was when we started wondering what we would do to return to our everyday lives again in Paradise.

We currently own an acre of land in Paradise, California, and we also have water on the first half acre, septic, septic, and electricity. We certainly could not afford another 2,400-square-foot home to be built. The only building we could afford would be a mobile home, which was still on backorder for up to a year or more. We were renting a home in Auburn, but we were not gaining any equity, and we were paying for someone else's mortgage, not our own. It was a lovely home; we enjoyed living there, but it wasn't ours. We would be unable to save much money to rebuild our home if we had to pay $2,400 a month for rent with no equity to show for it.

BJ and I looked at our options and decided to take the insurance money and put a down payment on a house to buy in Auburn so we would have someplace to live while waiting to rebuild on our acre of land in Paradise, California. We began looking in Auburn, a town like Paradise, for a house to buy to accommodate all three of us. We found a home in April that fit our needs quite well and was 2,400 square feet, with four bedrooms and three bathrooms. We decided to buy it to live in for at least two to five years until we hopefully got our settlement from PG&E. Given our age, this plan seemed the most responsible and feasible for us. BJ and Mom were already retired, and I was getting close to retirement age. We figured owning our home and land outright without a mortgage would be feasible for us to retire comfortably in Auburn or Paradise, California.

I decided to try to find another job as I had before the fire, working in the hospital as a discharge planner case manager so that I could continue to put money into my retirement account to prepare for my retirement. I filled out at least three or four applications for case manager discharge planners with hospitals in and around Auburn, California. Still, because I had only worked for four months as a discharge planner case manager in Paradise, other hospitals were reluctant to hire me for lack of one year of experience. I finally found a hospital willing to take a chance on me again in Folsom, California, about thirty minutes from my rental house in Auburn. That job would be much better than the current one-hour commute in terrible highway traffic. I could take back roads to get to this new job, and the hospital was the same size as the hospital in Paradise. I was very honest with the director of case management and let him know what my experience was and that I only had four months of experience, and he was willing to train me. I felt like I was getting my life back to normal. I was very happy.

I began my new job in July 2019 and was looking forward to doing the kind of job I had been doing before the fire. I loved being a hospital case manager/discharge planner. I was making about the same amount of money as I did at Feather River Hospital in Paradise doing the same thing. It seemed like my life was returning to normal after such a rough time after the Camp Fire.

We bought and moved into our new home in Auburn in May 2019 and were very happy to be in our own home again. Our furniture fit well, and Mom was happy in her suite of rooms on one side of the upstairs, with BJ and me on the other side. I had my office space on the main floor, and we had plenty of space for entertainment and for Bridget, Bill, and our grandsons to visit. We even had a fenced-in backyard so their dog Pepper could come to visit with the family.

Life seemed to be returning to "normal," just like before the fire. I was relieved because I knew several people, I was working with on the day of the fire who had still been unable to return to work due to PTSD. I'm unsure if they felt life was too short to go back to work doing something they were no longer enjoying or what exactly. I was just glad I felt strong enough to return to work as a nurse.

I was getting up, going to work, and coming home; I ate dinner, went to bed, and did it all over again. I enjoyed our new home and was getting used to the new community. My family and I were trying to get established with new medical providers and assimilate into the community. I quit my first post-Camp Fire job at Centene as a telephonic Medi-Cal RN Case Manager to re-establish myself in the same job I did before the fire. I was going back to in-hospital case management, more commonly known as a discharge planner. I truly enjoyed being an in-hospital case manager and was looking forward to returning to it and only having a thirty-minute commute.

My new job was starting in July, and I was going to start with an orientation and then do some training with this hospital's electronic medical records and systems. Orientation is usually non-stressful and somewhat dull, but it's necessary for any new job. I would work full-time during the orientation and training to finish it as soon as possible. Once orientation was finished, I planned to work as a per diam nurse until a part-time position became available, which my new director assured me would be available soon. As a per diam nurse, I would not have any medical benefits, so I decided to find my benefits and pay for them independently until the actual benefited position became available.

As my orientation and training for my new job as an in-hospital case manager came to an end, I asked my director for a couple of weeks of extra orientation because I was feeling a little unsure about the new system and wanted to be sure I was doing everything correctly before I was on my own. I knew something was wrong when I was told I should know how to do this job because I had done it before. I reminded my new director that I had told him I was unfamiliar with the utilization review part of this job because we had an outside agency who took over that piece of the job for us in my previous job at Feather River Hospital. He then remembered that conversation and agreed to the extra two weeks.

Working as an in-hospital case manager for the Paradise Feather River Hospital was a high-stress job. Still, it made the day go by fast, and I enjoyed working with patients and their families and working with such a wonderful group of teammates. We worked very well together, and no one on our team felt he or she was above any other team member, including doctors and managers.

This new job was different. I noticed that the team was working well, but the director needed to encourage the team. He was argumentative and condescending to many members of the group. Most of the team members were travel nurses, and about five full-time employees were currently on a leave of absence. This was not my first job in healthcare, and I am used to stressful jobs as an RN. I have been an RN for 36 years and have worked in the hospital, in-home health care, hospice, and long-term care, as well as in nursing education and leadership. I was no stranger to stress on the job, but something was different now, and I could not figure out what it was. I didn't seem to want to put up with stressful situations as I had done before.

I was finally left on my own off orientation a lot sooner than was supposed to happen, but again, in nursing, that's not unusual. I tried to make the best of a bad situation and muddle through as best as possible. I completed my day's work, stumbled home exhausted, and felt something was wrong about this situation. Usually, I would have complained to my family but just chalked it up to that's just the way nursing is and would have gone back for more of the same the following day. After all, this is what healthcare and nursing especially are like. After 36 years as a nurse, I knew the drill and knew that no other profession would allow this type of abusive behavior to happen not just for a day but for years. I had been indoctrinated into believing that abusiveness from a boss, from leadership in general, and from patients and their families is normal, and we learn to live with it. If we do not learn to live with it, we can find ourselves out of a job with another nurse more willing to put up with abuse and unsafe situations just waiting to step in. This time, something happened to me. I just snapped. I cannot explain what happened except to say I could not take it any longer. I was no longer willing to endure bad situations and abusive behavior. I had enough.

One day, I went home exhausted and decided to take a shower to help me relax; before I knew it, I was on the shower floor, crying and feeling like I couldn't go on. I also found myself reliving the fire and the day of the fire. I could not get out of the bottom of the shower, and I could not stop crying.

The more I thought about what had happened and how I reacted to what, up to that point, had been a very everyday occurrence in the world of hospital nursing, I realized something had changed in me. I became angry and decided to fight for myself if no one else would fight for me. No one, especially not a member of the healthcare profession who was diligently doing their job as I had been doing for the last 36 years, deserved to be treated with abuse by anyone. Not only was that unprofessional, but it was also just plain wrong.

I decided to talk to the HR department about what I had been through, and if necessary, I would quit my job effective immediately. No one deserved to be put in such a compromising position. I was sent to a new hospital unit where I had never been before and where it was understaffed and without enough help to do the job safely with a boss who blamed his subordinates for something we had no control over and that was his job to change.

I went to the HR department with my resignation and told them exactly what had been happening in our department. I told them that five other nurses from the same department were on stress-related leave of absence, which should tell them something about this department. I spoke with the HR director and let her know that this type of situation was not okay and that if that situation were not dealt with, more nurses would quit. I felt so very good after doing that. I realized I had changed. I was no longer the same person I was before the fire.

I realized that I was unsure if I still wanted to be a nurse or even wanted to be in healthcare. The one thing I did know for sure was that I was tired. At first, I thought I might be depressed, but I asked myself all the usual questions about feeling helpless or hopeless. I decided I was not feeling helpless or hopeless, but I was tired. I needed a rest. I knew I needed to work to help support my family, but at what?

I spoke with my husband about this because he was with me during my colossal meltdown. He was so very supportive, but at the same time, he was worried about finances, too. He was retired and collecting a pension and social security, but it was insufficient to support us. My mother was retired and was only getting meager social security. We had filed a lawsuit against PG&E but had yet to hear much about that and kept having to give our attorney more information to make our case against PG&E. The lawsuit was moving very slowly.

Despite all the financial issues we were facing, I still knew I needed to be true to myself and my needs. I was not willing to compromise myself anymore. I felt I survived for a reason, and that reason was not just to let other people walk all over me. I also no longer enjoyed doing the things I did before the fire. I used to knit and crochet, but I had no interest in doing that anymore. I also used to like to do different craft projects, but I did not want to do those either. I did not have knitting needles, crochet hooks, or crafting supplies, and I did not want to buy them. I had been keeping a journal and thought about writing about the fire but did not know where to start. I felt stuck. I decided I needed to go back into therapy. I began looking for a new therapist to help me deal with the trauma from the fire and how that trauma was now affecting my life in the future. I needed help understanding how my life had changed and what that new reality looked like for me.

As I was taking a much-needed rest, I got a call from a recruiter for Adventist Health. Months ago, I had filled out a job application for them as a case manager or utilization review nurse but had never heard anything. They had kept my resume and application on file, however. They were now calling me with an offer for an interview at their Roseville corporate headquarters as a utilization review nurse for their employee health plan benefits department. I would not look a gift horse in the mouth, so I agreed to the interview.

I went to the interview in Roseville, California, at the Adventist Health Benefits Administration office building on Creekside Road. The following week, I was offered the job. I accepted the job as a utilization review nurse for the Adventist Health Employee Health Plan. I was back working in managed care, but it was perfect. Even though I was working full time, I was working only thirty minutes from my house and did not even have to go on the freeway to get to my job. The job was less stressful than hospital case management, and my boss seemed lovely. The whole team was so nice to work with.

I was still looking for a therapist, but in the meantime, I needed to work, and even though I was not sure I still wanted to work as a nurse, I could work as a utilization review nurse and only have to speak with doctors and patients and their families over the phone. It seemed like an excellent job for the time being, and it paid well enough and had the benefits I needed. I was also happy to be back working for Adventist Health again.

As I worked at my new job, I realized I still enjoyed being a nurse. I just had not enjoyed being mistreated as a nurse. I also realized that I enjoyed working telephonically and that I liked having a desk job for the time being. I used to think desk jobs were too dull and never liked them in the past, but now it was right up my alley. I had a much lower tolerance for stress and abuse than I used to.

After working for the Adventist Health Benefits Administration Department for a few months, I spoke with the behavioral health case manager, Linda. I asked her for a list of therapists with experience in post-traumatic stress disorder. I was given a list of about three to five names of therapists in my area of Auburn, California. I called the first three names and left messages. One of the providers called me back right away, and I explained to her what I was looking for. She agreed to see me, but not until next month. Mental health providers are in high demand and in short supply all over. I was not surprised at having to wait.

I finally saw my new therapist, Pat, and was very pleased with her. Pat listened to me and not only helped me to deal with more of my PTSD symptoms, but she also helped me understand my changing behavior and how I had indeed changed from the person I had been to the person I am now. She was understanding and insightful, and I needed that. She helped me to see that I needed to get in touch with how I was feeling and to listen to my feelings. She also helped me understand that my feelings were not wrong or right, but they just were. She even gave me homework assignments to do. One assignment was to sit on a beach somewhere and do nothing. Pat gave me permission to rest. She also taught me that average was a moving target. What is normal for one person may not be typical for another. It is essential to find what feels suitable for me, and if it doesn't hurt anyone else, I should do what seems right for me. I told her I was unsure what I enjoyed or did not enjoy doing anymore. Pat said I should try doing things and ask myself if I wanted to keep doing them, and if not, try something else.

After just a few sessions with Pat, I decided to try doing some crafts I had never done before. I tried jewelry making and found I enjoyed it. I also bought new knitting needles and yarn and began knitting again. I enjoyed both. I realized I do not enjoy cooking. I told my husband I never liked cooking, and he said he did, so he now cooks.

My life is different from before the fire because I am different. I do not think anyone can go through such a traumatic event and almost die and not be changed by the experience. I think everyone who goes through a traumatic event is forever altered by it. I certainly have changed from the person I was before the fire, and I cannot and will not go back.

The most significant change I have made has been paying more attention to myself and my needs. I use the word "no" more than I did in the past. If I do not want to do something, I speak up. Also, I agree to do things I might have said no to because I had never done it before and did not feel comfortable doing it. I take chances to do things I might not have done before. Another thing I started doing is acknowledging when I do something well, and I pay attention to people when they give me compliments and accept those compliments by saying "thank you." I have tried to stop making excuses or refusing a compliment. I stopped taking myself for granted. Part of finding my new normal is finding out about the new me. It's a work in progress.

CHAPTER 20

CAMP FIRE LESSONS LEARNED

L ooking back over the whole Camp Fire disaster, I felt it was essential to review it for the lessons that my family and I learned to pass on these lessons to you, the reader, to help change things for the better for the next wildfire disaster to come along, because it will. Below are lessons we learned that will help others when wildfire hits another Wildland Urban Interface Community. These lessons learned are in no particular order; take what you like and leave the rest.

1. We never put our printed pictures or photo albums onto an electronic device. So, we lost any photos not on our phones or our computers. I have no photos of my daughter, grandsons, or family that were not on my cell phone or computer before the fire. This includes my wedding photos and my daughter's wedding photos. **Lesson learned: Back up all photo album pictures onto several electronic devices and store them on the cloud if you lose the photos.**

2. We had no extra change of clothes in our cars. It would have been nice to have a change that I knew fit me and would at least be comfortable. **Lesson**

learned: **Pack a to-go bag with a change of clothes, shoes, and some food and water with a pre-paid credit card in it and keep it in your car in case you have to evacuate quickly.**

3. Before the fire, we never looked carefully at our homeowners or auto insurance policies. We thought we had enough insurance but could have had more of both. We also never really looked at the fine print, which is now becoming a problem with reimbursing the State of California for the debris removal cost.

The state removed all the toxic debris from our land after the fire and said we would not have to pay it back if our insurance company didn't cover debris removal. If it did provide funds for debris removal, the state wanted to be reimbursed.

We read our homeowner's insurance policy, but not well enough.

Our policy gave us $17,000 for landscape and tree replacement and another $23,000 for outbuilding replacement or repair. We saw nothing about debris removal, so we thought our policy didn't provide for that and we would not have to reimburse the State of California for it. Unfortunately, in the fine print, after each section about the landscape and tree replacement money and the outbuilding repair and replacement money, it read that if we had to have debris removal, the outbuilding repair and replacement and the landscape and tree replacement money were to be used for debris removal. We now owe $40,000 to the State of California for debris removal reimbursement. **Lesson learned: Check your insurance policy fine print and then call your agent to ensure you have not missed anything.**

4. We found we were alone for thirty days after the Camp Fire disaster. No one gave us hotel vouchers or gave us any toiletries or changes of clothes after we escaped from the fire. No one helped us out of the fire zone. We got ourselves out. Even when we got to the hospital in Chico, and I was seen in the ER there, I was not given any place to stay or clothes to change into. I was discharged, given an antibiotic prescription, and told to "take care of myself." Neither the Federal Emergency Management Agency (FEMA) nor the Red Cross had reached the Camp Fire disaster area yet. All the hotels for miles were packed up, and we had no family in the area to go to for help. Our house was gone, we had to evacuate the area, and we had nowhere to go. The only emergency shelters were being set up at churches, and there were not many of them, and they could not hold 52,000 people. **Lesson learned: After a considerable fire-related disaster or any large disaster, you are on your own for at least two weeks to 30 days.**

5. Your insurance agent is not necessarily your friend or your enemy. You have paid for your insurance, so don't be afraid to use it. You will need it, and you are entitled to it. You are responsible for knowing what your policy covers and does not cover and reading all the fine print. Call your insurance agent as soon as possible after any disaster or accident. **Lesson learned: The sooner you file a claim, the faster you get your money.**

6. Almost everything burns to ashes in a fire, even in a safe. Our daughter and son-in-law had valuables in a supposedly fireproof safe. The safe was fireproof and didn't burn, but everything in it burned to ash

because the fire was so hot it cooked what was in the safe as if it were an oven. Only ashes were left, and if any paper was left, it crumbled to ash as soon as it was touched. **Lesson learned: Take pictures of all your valuables and furniture before a disaster strikes. This will make filing your claim more accessible and less refutable by the insurance company. A picture is worth a thousand words.**

7. When FEMA, the Red Cross, and the National Guard come, let them know what you need most and give them a list. Be prepared to argue with them. They do go to many disasters and have their way of doing things. One of the things we needed in Paradise was housing, and FEMA did have trailers for housing that they brought with them. Still, they insisted the community let them know where they could set them up, and the community had to find land to put the trailers on that had a sewer hookup and water and electricity hookups. None of the trailers were made available until a place to put them with their exact specifications was provided. Our community had a hard time finding a place to put the trailers, and FEMA and the Red Cross insisted on closing all but three shelters that FEMA was running, and the Red Cross with the National Guard. FEMA finally found a place to put the trailers, but they had to pay rent on the land to get it. If you have a disaster plan for your community, have a copy ready and give it to FEMA and the Red Cross to work with. Don't assume FEMA, the National Guard, or the Red Cross knows more than you do. Yes, they do this a lot, but not in your community. **Lesson learned: You know your community best. Hold your ground and ask**

for what you want and what you need, even from all the disaster relief organizations.

8. Help is only available to the needy in any community, as it should be. FEMA will have housing and monetary assistance, which will be given out based on income needs. Most people will only qualify for a low-interest loan of 3% up to the maximum of $200,000. Only very low-income families or individuals will be eligible for housing like trailers or money for twelve months. **Lesson learned: After twelve months, FEMA assistance ends, and you must find your housing and funds, such as Medi-Cal or Cal Fresh in California.**

9. Most people want to give money to a problem to keep themselves from feeling bad. Let them. You need money to help you through this challenging time, and people want to help. It's a win-win. Swallow your pride and accept their help. If it makes you feel better, give money back to others the next time a disaster strikes, and you are back on your feet again. We received many different gift cards and checks from different organizations when we were without a home or belongings. We were grateful and have since given that money back in charitable ways. I give part of my paycheck to a fund we started at Adventist Health for associates in need. I was once one of those associates, and I know how vital that fund is to people in need. I have more than given back what I received, but I still give. **Lesson learned: Allow people to help you. They need to help you, so let them.**

10. Our mortgage company and auto loan bank were willing to help us. All we needed to do was sign a

couple of forms. Even if you have the money to make your payments, I recommend you do this to keep yourself fluid with cash, at least for the first thirty days after the disaster. You may need it. If you need to find another place to live, you may need a deposit for a rental property, VRBO, or Airbnb while your property is repaired or the insurance is settled. **Lesson learned: If you are out of work and waiting for your insurance reimbursement for your homeowner's insurance or your auto insurance, ask your mortgage company for a deferment. They are usually willing to help you, and they were willing to give us one for three to six months after the fire until the insurance could settle our claims.**

11. We were very happy that we had a credit card or two with higher limits. We used those for the hotel we stayed in for a while. During the first thirty days, the insurance was trying to figure out how much of a housing allowance we would get, and they were not willing to pay us but instead paid a third party to pay the hotel directly. This took a few weeks to arrange, and, in the meantime, we paid our hotel bills and the insurance company reimbursed us, but we had to show them our receipts. We had to pay for food for three meals a day, and we ate out because we were staying in a hotel. We also had to buy clothes, shoes, coats, toiletries, and hygiene supplies. It added up. I first lost my credit cards in the fire, but luckily, my husband had his. I recommend a joint credit card with a high spending limit. We had one that earned us travel points, so we racked up the points and paid off our balance once the insurance money

started to come in. We needed a vacation after all this anyway. **Lesson learned: Always have either a pre-paid credit card you can keep adding money to or always have a credit card with a high credit limit on you or with you. It comes in handy during a disaster.**

12. When you first move into a new area, sign up for the disaster alert system. Sometimes, it's called a civil defense or disaster early warning system. This way, you will be notified of an issue in your area. Yes, you will get many alerts, but at least you won't miss anything. We didn't do that in Paradise because we didn't know about it or get any warning about the fire before it was upon us. **Lesson learned: Always sign up for your community's disaster alert system. Do that as one of the first things you do when you move to a new community.**

13. Many people were left without medications during the fire's aftermath. Their doctors' offices or clinics were destroyed with all their records. We had to get replacement prescriptions. I was on high blood pressure medication and heart anti-arrhythmia medication, and my husband was on medication for COPD. My mom had thyroid medication and high blood pressure medication as well. In my case and my mother's case, we went to urgent care or the ER and were given a replacement prescription with refills good for three months. This gave us time to find a new provider in a new community or for our old providers to reestablish in a different area of Butte County. It's a good short-term solution, but it is only a short-term solution. **Lesson learned: If you need replacement medications and don't have**

a primary care doctor after a disaster, you can go to an urgent care clinic, or if you need the ER, you can ask for replacement medication prescriptions.

14. As I said in the book, my husband and I kept our important family papers in a metal file box with a lock. We keep all our important papers, such as insurance policies, birth certificates, marriage certificates, tax returns for the previous year, medication lists, etc. You get the idea. Anything you will need to help recover quickly after a disaster. **Lesson learned: Keep essential papers in an easily grabbed fire-resistant and or water-resistant box or online on the cloud.**

15. One piece of insurance we did not have and wished we did was collectible insurance. This type of insurance differs from personal possessions in a regular homeowner's or renter's insurance policy. Collectible insurance is insurance that art collectors or stamp collectors might have. You need collectible insurance if you have a collection of anything worth anything. My husband had an O gage railroad train collection, and we had a professional photographer print by famous photographer Peter Lik. When we bought the Peter Lik print, we paid $3,500; at the time of the fire, the print would have been worth $8,000. Collectible insurance will pay you the current market value of the collection, so if you want to, you can replace it and not be out any money. A regular insurance policy lumps the collection in with your possessions and doesn't pay current market value for them. We could not afford to replace my husband's train set or the print. We no longer have any collectibles, but we would have the

proper insurance to replace them if we did. **Lesson learned: Buy collectible insurance if you have any collectibles. Regular homeowner's or renter's insurance won't cover the cost of replacing a collectible at its current value.**

16. We learned how important it was for us to leave the disaster area after the fire. Not only were we able to get better air quality, but we were also able to find a hotel. Many people are displaced at once during a large disaster like the Camp Fire. In our case, 52,000 people were displaced in less than twenty-four hours. This puts a significant strain on the surrounding communities to pick up the displaced population and thus causes increased stress for everyone. Getting out of the disaster area allows you time to recover and destress. You also have more resources that you don't have to share with the other displaced people. **Lesson learned: Leave the disaster area as soon as possible after the disaster and go back to visit the area for insurance issues or to deal with any property issues. You will need a respite from the disaster.**

17. You want to find a trauma therapist and one who is familiar with trauma or PTSD therapy. Most healthcare insurance companies have mental health providers; you can look them up and ask them if they do PTSD trauma therapy. I just googled trauma therapy and counseling to find my therapist. I chose three therapists and called them. I asked them about their experience with trauma therapy, told them what I had been through briefly, and decided to go to whoever could get me in soon. After the immediate EMDR therapy I went through to help

me with the worst PTSD, I chose another therapist under my insurance for further therapy. Many times, after a large disaster, trauma counselors are mobilized to help in the immediate aftermath of the disaster. They will take any victims needing trauma therapy immediately at no cost. You can contact the disaster relief centers to find out about them or google the disaster, and many resources are listed, including trauma therapy. **Lesson learned: Start trauma therapy for the post-traumatic stress disorder (PTSD) you will have as soon as possible. You will need it.**

18. It is very important that you have access to your mail after a disaster. Many insurance companies send forms to you for you to fill out and sign. Now we have e-mail and DocuSign, but we did not have that when the Camp Fire hit. See if you can get a PO box or ask a friend if you can have your mail forwarded to their home so you can pick it up off and on throughout the week or ask your friend or relative to call you when anything comes for you in the mail. Our mail was forwarded to my aunt's house in Dublin, CA. We just went to the post office collecting our mail for us during the fire, the Chico main post office, and gave them my aunt's address as our forwarding address and got our mail that way. It was much easier than driving to Chico weekly to pick up our mail. **Lesson learned: Have your mail forwarded to a friend or family member if you don't have a house yet as soon as you can after the disaster so you don't miss any mail.**

19. If you can afford a hotel room or have somewhere else to go, don't go to a shelter. Shelters become

overcrowded fast and should be reserved for those people who cannot afford to go anywhere else but a shelter. One of the issues faced during the Camp Fire was that the shelters filled up quickly and were overcrowded. There was an outbreak of Norovirus in each of them due to overcrowding. The shelters do what they can and try not to turn anyone away unless necessary, so if you don't need to go to one, don't. **Lesson learned: Stay out of the disaster shelters as much as possible. They quickly get overcrowded. Leave them for those who genuinely need help.**

20. As I mentioned earlier in the book, one of the saddest stories was about my friend and fellow nurse, Nichole, who had three horses but only had a horse trailer for two horses. Luckily, they could get all three horses out safely using a friend's trailer, but I recommend having a pet carrier for each pet you own. Even if your pet isn't used to being in a carrier during a disaster, they will want to be in one, and you will also want them in it. Your pets will feel more secure, you will know where they are, and they will be easily accessible. **Lesson learned: Always have a pet carrier or trailer for every pet you have.**

21. The next thing that goes along with the item above is if your pet is hiding and won't come out or it runs away, don't spend precious time looking for it or trying to coax it out of hiding. Some of the deaths in the Camp Fire were due to the owners of pets taking precious time trying to get their pets, and they all lost their lives. Let your pet do what it needs to do. Animals are much more resilient than we are in a disaster. Leave a window or door open or a pet door open for it to get out of the house after you leave,

and if the pet runs away, let it go and look for it after the disaster is over. Believe me. People will care for your pet if you are not in the area. During the Camp Fire, we had shelters for pets; people rescued pets that ran away from their owners because they were scared, only to be found hungry but safe a day or more later. Nothing is sadder than a pet without an owner because the owner was looking for their pet and was killed in the fire. Then what does the pet do later? You need to live. Your pet will live, or it won't, but it will have a much better chance at survival than you will. Many pet owners in the Camp Fire were reunited with their pets' days and weeks after the fire, and luckily, both were well. **Lesson learned: If your pet won't come to you and is hiding, ensure it can get outside and let it go. Save yourself. Your pet can get out of a disaster area more easily than you can.**

22. After returning to the hospital because I couldn't escape right away, I learned that sometimes you need to shelter in place. **Lesson learned: If you can't evacuate safely because the fire is all around you, look for water and go to it, or look for a large, unvegetated area with little to no trees and go there in your car. Stay in your car; don't get out unless it's on fire. You have protection in your car, at least from the embers flying in the air.**

23. Don't wait to be told to leave if you know the fire is headed your way. Leave as soon as possible. If you don't need to evacuate, you can always return when the fire is out. **Lesson learned: The sooner you evacuate, the better because it gets as many**

drivers as possible off the road early so there is no traffic jam when the fire is at its worst.

24. My family and I decided to meet at Enloe Hospital in Chico in the case of the Camp Fire. Don't be a hero and try to stay to defend your home. Your home is not worth your life. You are important to the survival of your family. They need you to live. The best practice is to have a 100-foot perimeter of no vegetation around your house. In that case, you have a metal roof or fire-retardant shingles, no trees close to your house to burn, and no wood fencing around your house to cause embers to go into your attic. All your doors and windows are closed when you leave; you have done all you can do. If the fire gets into your house, it will probably burn, and no matter what you try to do to prevent it, it's not worth losing your life. **Lesson learned: Plan what you and your family will do and how you will evacuate in the event of a wildfire. If you are separated from each other, decide where you will meet up, well away from the fire area.**

25. In a wildfire, a lot of smoke, toxic substances, and particles are in the air. Those substances can cause anyone with breathing difficulty or heart disease to be at risk for stress-related illnesses, heart attacks, strokes, and asthma attacks. Also, if someone is at risk for mental illness, look for increased depression or suicidal ideations. Within 30–60 days after the Camp Fire, several elderly people I knew suffered heart attacks, strokes, and other stress-related illnesses and died. Their deaths have not been directly attributed to the Camp Fire but, in my opinion, should be. My mother collapsed two days after the

fire due to stress and had to go to the hospital. Don't treat post-traumatic stress lightly. **Lesson learned: After a disaster, watch yourself, your family, and other victims for signs of stress-related illnesses such as heart attack or stroke. Stress, such as what happens in a disaster, can push someone over the edge who might be predisposed to heart disease, stroke, or respiratory illness.**

26. I don't think you can bounce back right away. If you need to rest, then rest. If you need to get away for a while, then do that. There is no right or wrong way to recover from trauma. The only wrong way is not to recover. My husband and I had a vacation planned for January to Florida to visit friends; we went. It was one of the best ideas we had. We were able to come back with a fresh perspective and well-rested. **Lesson learned: My most important lesson is to cut myself slack. Any traumatic experience is complex, and the stress it causes is natural.**

CHAPTER 21

CONCLUSION

I t's been just about five years since the Paradise, CA,
Camp Fire destroyed our home, my car, my place of
business, and 95% of the town of Paradise, CA. Our
town was just the first town destroyed by such a wildfire,
but it is not the last. I want to say that the United States
has learned lessons in response to wildfire disasters and
has improved how it responds. Unfortunately, it has not.
At the completion of my story of survival and recovery
from a devastating wildfire, another community's story
is just beginning.

Although a disaster can end your life as you know it,
your life can continue. It may not be the life you knew
before the disaster, but it will continue. My family and I
had a wonderful life before the Camp Fire destroyed our
home and our lives as we knew them, but thank God we
survived. I miss some of my stuff, but not all of it, and I
would never have missed stuff over people ever.

We don't have the lives we had before the fire, but
we have lives that have taken a different path. I think I
will feel like a refugee for a while still, and every night,
I pray I will have all the resources I need to stay on this
new path God has provided me with. I believe He saved

me, my family, and all of us Camp Fire survivors for a reason. I hope to discover the reason one day soon.

My husband and I are getting older, and at the age of sixty-two, I plan on retiring from my job as a case manager for the Adventist Health Employee Health Plan. While I enjoyed my forty years as a registered nurse, times are changing, and health care needs to change with the times. I'm too tired and worn down to continue fighting for the needed changes.

My family and I now live in a much smaller house than we did in Paradise, California. We may never be able to live in the size house we had then, but I love living in my little thirteen-hundred-square-foot house on the Big Island of Hawaii. We live on an island surrounded by water, and we live on the rainy side of the island in a tropical rainforest, and I finally feel safe.

Climate change is real. Science is clear for anyone who wants to see and believe it.

I won't convince anyone one way or another that climate change is real; frankly, I don't want to waste my time trying. Either you believe the science that says it's real, or you don't. It is all up to each individual person to believe it or not. I can and did tell you what it was like in the deadliest wildfire in California. If what I wrote doesn't help to convince you to believe and make plans to change your lives accordingly, I don't know what will.

I had never seen a fire that behaved like the Camp Fire before it occurred, but I have since. Climate change is the only explanation I can come up with for how fast and hot that fire burned and how long it burned. If God didn't intercede with rain, I don't know how many more acres would have burned or how many more communities would have been destroyed. Over 150,000 acres were burned that day, 18,000 buildings were destroyed, 52,000 people were displaced, and 85 died in the Camp Fire on November 8th, 2018.

Many other towns have felt and will feel the effects of massive wildfire destruction. Many buildings and people have been displaced, destroyed, and killed in California and worldwide. Climate change will continue to occur, causing more weather-related disasters regardless of whether you believe it's real. It will continue to affect everything, from weather changes and increased wildfires to increased poor air quality in the United States and worldwide. It has become the norm for bigger and bigger natural disasters to occur more often than ever before.

At the completion of this book, the town of Lahaina Maui, Hawaii, has been destroyed by wildfire, and the death toll has reached 114 so far, according to the news. Lahaina, on the west side of Maui, Hawaii, had stood since the 1800s and was once a thriving whaling town turned into a very prosperous tourist town until it was destroyed by a wildfire fanned by winds caused by a Pacific cyclone storm passing to the south of Hawaii. The storm itself was not a problem, but the winds were. Even though the storm passed well to the south of Hawaii, the winds were still strong enough to fan the flames of the fire, making its own wind that reached over 80 miles an hour and causing such devastation. Many people ran to the ocean to escape the flames and then had to be rescued by the Coast Guard as they clung to anything they could to remain afloat. Some didn't survive.

Science is clear that climate change is real, and disasters will continue to worsen, not improve. We will need a new way to manage and respond to the new types of large-scale disasters produced by climate change. We will need to pre-plan for disasters that will happen by having a plan already in place and ready to go that can be implemented immediately. Since the Camp Fire, I have given this problem much thought. In health care, we tend to think ahead, with a more systematic approach to problems, and plan for problems before they happen rather than after the fact. As a case manager, I look at patients and their problems holistically. Keeping this in mind, I used my skills as a case manager, as a nurse of forty years, and as a major disaster survivor to help me develop an out-of-the-box solution to disaster response management. While I don't believe this plan is the end-all or be-all, I think it's a place to start. This plan is predicated on developing a disaster team that can go to the disaster area or as close as possible and set up all the needed components, such as evacuation centers, disaster relief centers, food, clothing, water, bathing, and bathroom facilities as well as trauma counseling and anything else needed by disaster survivors.

This disaster response plan should be set up and training put in place by the National Guard, the Army, the Air Force, and the Navy. All military branches are well-trained in the immediate setup and response to a war situation, and honestly, what is a disaster but another type of war? We need to be able to get the survivors out of the disaster area quickly so the disaster area can be secured and the danger removed, and this cannot happen if survivors are in the way. Being a disaster survivor, I can tell you firsthand the importance of getting away from the disaster area as quickly as possible to destress and heal from some of the trauma before tackling all the new issues that such a devastating loss entails. We also need to have state and maybe even county preset-up supplies of food, clothing, water, medicines, and any other potentially needed supplies in a safe place before a disaster occurs. In this way, the disaster team can be sent to the disaster site and have all needed supplies already there for them to distribute as needed.

We need a way to go into a disaster zone as close to the disaster as that is safe enough and set up essentially a field hospital with places for disaster evacuees to be treated to provide rest and all the basic needs they will require while recovering to the point that they can begin again with their new lives.

Below are my plan suggestions and recommendations encompassing my idea for a federal, state, and regional disaster management response plan. My plan consists of having four different regional disaster response teams for the country's Western, Mountain, Central, and Eastern regions. This disaster response plan will have federal and state funding. It will be a new department in the federal and state governments called the Disaster Response Management Department. I propose a new type of insurance that all U.S. citizens will need to have, and that is disaster insurance. The Federal Insurance Commission should manage this insurance. The insurance should be paid by citizens like a payroll tax and taken out of paychecks as Social Security or Medicare is. Everyone in the United States would be entitled to assistance during a disaster. We all donate to disaster victims and have telethons to try to help the victims of disaster anyway; this is a pre-paid plan we all pay into to fund the program before it's needed. We need to plan instead of having to set up disaster responses after the disaster occurs when we are already behind the eight ball, so to speak.

The disaster response plan below is only a suggestion as a starting point. It is not meant to be the end-all and be-all. It's one idea. What's another one?

RECOMMENDATION FOR A FEDERAL & STATE DISASTER RESPONSE MANAGEMENT PROGRAM

Federal Government will create a new federally mandated insurance for disasters. Paid by all citizens living in the US based on income.

New Department Creation by the Federal Government called the Department of Disaster Response Management, and Congress will appoint the Director.

FEMA will be part of the new department and reabsorbed into the new program.

The new department will be separated into regions to consider the different regional variations and types of possible disasters. Headed by regional directors.

Each region will review the state disaster plans in its region and create a regional plan. Then it will create disaster response teams for each region. The teams will go to any state in the region where a disaster occurs. The supplies needed will already be in place in each region waiting for the team to arrive at the disaster site to distribute the needed supplies. (Supplies provided to each region by the federal government).

Federal Government

Director of Disaster Response Management		Deputy Director of Disaster Response Management	
Western Regional Director of Emergency Response Planning	Mountain Regional Director of Emergency Response Planning	Central Regional Director of Emergency Response Planning	Eastern Regional Director of Emergency Response Planning
Regional Dept. of Emergency Response Planning Western States incuding Hawaii and Alaska	Regional Dept. of Empergency Response Planning Mountain States	Regional Dept. of Emergency Response Planning Central States Emergency Response Planning	Regional Dept.of Emergency Response Planning Eastern States Emergency Response Planning
Western Region Disaster Response Team	Mountain Region Disaster Responce Team	Central Region Disaster Response Team	Eastern Regional Disaster Response Teams
Manage Disaster Relief Centers & Evacuation Centers & LT Housing of evacuees & Replacement Centers	Manage Disaster Relief Centers & Evacuation Centers & LT Housing of evacuees & Replacement Centers	Manage Disaster Relief Centers & Evacuation Centers & LT Housing of evacuees Replacement Centers	Manage Disaster Relief Centers & Evacuation Centers & LT Housing of evacuees & Replacement Centers

Each team will assist with the evacuation of the disaster area by providing evacuation centers outside of the disaster area with disaster centers that have beds, bathing facilities, bathroom facilities, food, housing, clothing, counseling, replacement document centers, mail forwarding, medical care, and replacement centers for housewares, furniture, and initial home set up items. Long-term housing assistance will also be provided. They will also record evacuees, missing persons, and mortalities. They will provide temporary pet housing and will provide childcare services.

THE END

REFERENCES

1. https://www.nytimes.com/interactive/2018/11/18/us/california-camp-fire-paradise.html
2. News Article in Wildfire Today.: Estimated TOTAL cost of the Camp Fire was about $422 billion. https://wildfiretoday.com/2021/11/21/acres-burned-in-lower-49-states-this-year-is-more-than-average/
3. FEMA: https://www.usfa.fema.gov/wui/what-is-the-wui.html
4. NOAA (National Oceanic and Atmospheric Administration). 2022. Billion-dollar weather and climate disasters. www.ncei.noaa.gov/access/billions.
5. History of the Town of Paradise, CA, https://www.citytowninfo.com/places/california/paradis
6. Trauma Recovery EMDR Humanitarian Assistance Programs; https://www.emdrhap.org
7. https://my.clevelandclinic.org/health/treatments/22641-emdr-therapy#:~:text=Eye%20movement%20desensitization%20and%20reprocessing%20(EMDR)%20therapy%20is%20a%20mental,or%20other%20distressing%20life%20experiences
8. https://www.nytimes.com/interactive/2018/11/18/us/california-camp-fire-paradise.html
9. https://www.fire.ca.gov/our-impact/remembering-the-camp-fire

DOCUMENTARIES ABOUT THE CAMP FIRE

1. *Fire in Paradise* on Netflix
2. *Rebuilding Paradise* on National Geographic Chanel and ABC

RESOURCES FOR WILDFIRE AND OTHER DISASTER SURVIVORS

1. United Way: Free, confidential, and accessible 24/7 for people across the United States to find local resources.related to SDOH (e.g., housing, food, disaster assistance): www.211.org
2. Find Help: Offers free and reduced-cost U.S. zip [1] code-based community services search tools: www. findhelp.org.
3. National Center for Medical-Legal Partnership: Embeds legal professionals in healthcare teams to help address legal issues related to housing, utilities, employment, education, legal status, etc.: www. medical-legalpartnership.org
4. Health Leads: Free health advocates to connect. patients to local community resources through a growing national network: www.healthleadsusa.org
5. Single Stop: Social service locator that uses technology to connect people to resources across 17 states: https://singlestop.org.
6. Red Cross- www.redcross.org; Retrieved 9/18/19.
7. Aunt Bertha for Reduced cost services www. auntbertha.com
8. Federal Emergency Management Agency (FEMA)- www.fema.gov

9. Healthwise- Post-Traumatic Stress Disorder; Purifying Your Drinking Water https://www. helathwise.net Retrieved 9/18/19.
10. Catholic Charities: https://catholiccharitiesusa.org/ Retrieved 11/03/19.
11. 11. Administration for Children and Families (ACF) https://www.acttpf.hhs.gov/ohser/response_ recovery/acf-capabilities; Retrieved Oct. 1st, 2019.
12. 12. The US Department of Homeland Security; https://www.dhs.gov/disaster; Retrieved Oct 1st, 2019.
13. 13. Disaster Unemployment Assistance (DUA) https://www.dol.gov/ https://oui.doleta.gov/ unemploy/disaster.asp; Retrieved Nov. 3, 2019.

Made in the USA
Middletown, DE
24 September 2024

61290328R00088